Low for Long?
Causes and Consequences of
Persistently Low Interest Rates

Geneva Reports on the World Economy 17

International Center for Monetary and Banking Studies (ICMB)

International Center for Monetary and Banking Studies
2, Chemin Eugène-Rigot
1202 Geneva
Switzerland

Tel: (41 22) 734 9548
Fax: (41 22) 733 3853
Web: www.icmb.ch

Centre for Economic Policy Research

Centre for Economic Policy Research
3rd Floor
77 Bastwick Street
London EC1V 3PZ
UK

Tel: +44 (20) 7183 8801
Fax: +44 (20) 7183 8820
Email: cepr@cepr.org
Web: www.cepr.org

ISBN: 978-1-907142-94-9

Low for Long?
Causes and Consequences of Persistently Low Interest Rates

Geneva Reports on the World Economy 17

Charles Bean
London School of Economics and CEPR

Christian Broda
Duquesne Capital Management

Takatoshi Ito
University of Tokyo, University of Columbia and CEPR

Randall Kroszner
Booth School of Business, University of Chicago

ICMB **INTERNATIONAL CENTER FOR MONETARY AND BANKING STUDIES**
CIMB **CENTRE INTERNATIONAL D'ETUDES MONETAIRES ET BANCAIRES**

CEPR PRESS

About the Authors

Charles Bean is a Professor of Economics at the London School of Economics. From 2000 to 2014, he served at the Bank of England as, successively, Executive Director and Chief Economist, and then Deputy Governor for Monetary Policy, in which capacity he was a member of the Monetary Policy and Financial Policy Committees. Before joining the Bank, he was a member of faculty at LSE and was Managing Editor of the *Review of Economic Studies*; he has also worked at HM Treasury. He was President of the Royal Economic Society from 2013 to 2015 and was knighted in 2014 for services to monetary policy and central banking. He holds a PhD from MIT.

Christian Broda is a Managing Director at Duquesne Capital Management. Prior to joining Duquesne, he was Professor of Economics at the University of Chicago. He has published numerous articles in leading economic journals and books on international finance and trade. He has also held positions at Lehman Brothers, as Chief International Economist; at Barclays Capital, as Head of International Research; at Columbia University; and at the Federal Reserve Bank of New York. He is an associate editor of the *Journal of Development Economics*, a faculty fellow of the National Bureau of Economic Research, and a co-editor of the *IMF Economic Review*. He received his PhD from MIT.

Takatoshi Ito is a Professor in the School of International and Public Affairs, Columbia University and Associate Director of Research at the Center on Japanese Economy and Business. He has also held academic positions at the Universities of Minnesota, Hitotsubashi and Tokyo. He has also served in the public sector, including as a Senior Advisor at the IMF; as Deputy Vice-Minister for International Affairs at the Ministry of Finance (1999-2001); and on the Prime Minister's Council on Economic and Fiscal Policy (2006-8). He is the author of several books on the Japanese economy and of more than 130 academic articles. He was President of the Japanese Economic Association in 2004 and was awarded the National Medal with Purple Ribbon in 2011 for academic achievement. He holds a PhD from Harvard University.

Randall S. Kroszner is the Norman R. Bobins Professor of Economics at the University of Chicago's Booth School of Business. From 2006 to 2009, he served as a Governor of the US Federal Reserve System, chairing the Fed's committees on Supervision and Regulation and on Consumer and Community Affairs. From 2001 to 2003, he was a member of the US President's Council of Economic Advisers. He has more than 100 publications to his name, including a recent book co-authored with Robert J. Shiller, *Reforming US Financial Markets: Reflections Before and Beyond Dodd-Frank*. He received his PhD from Harvard University.

Acknowledgements

The authors are most grateful for the many insightful comments received from the discussants and participants at the conference to discuss the first draft of this report.

Contents

List of Conference Participants

Ivan Adamovich — Member of the Executive Board
Notenstein Private Bank Ltd, Zürich

Philip Adler — Head of Capital Markets
Crédit Agricole (Suisse) SA, Geneva

Edmond Alphandéry — Chairman
Centre For European Policy Studies, Paris

Katrin Assenmacher — Head of Monetary Policy Analysis
Swiss National Bank, Zürich

Simone Auer — Economist
Swiss National Bank, Zürich

Richard Baldwin — Professor of International Economics
The Graduate Institute, Geneva
Director
CEPR, London

Vít Bárta — Advisor to Governor
Czech National Bank, Prague

Sir Charles Bean — Professor
London School of Economics

Agnès Bénassy-Quéré — Professor
Paris School of Economics
French Council of Economic Analysis, Paris

Mickael Benhaim — Co-Head of Global Bonds Fixed Income
Pictet Asset Management, Geneva

Jan Marc Berk — Director and Research Division
De Nederlandsche Bank NV

Rémy Bersier — Member of the Executive Board
Banque Julius Baer & Co. Ltd, Geneva

Robert Bichsel — Head of Banking System Financial Stability
Swiss National Bank, Bern

Laurence Boone	Counsellor at the Presidency of the French Republic International and European Economic and Financial Affairs Sherpa, Paris
Claudio Borio	Head of the Monetary and Economic Department Bank for International Settlements (BIS), Basel
Christian Broda	Managing Director Duquesne Family Office, New York
Luigi Buttiglione	Head of Global Strategy Brevan Howard Investment Products, Geneva
Olli Castren	Economist Strategy - Research Brevan Howard Investment Products, Geneva
Benoît Coeuré	Member of the Executive Board European Central Bank, Frankfurt
Philippe Communod	Head of Treasury Crédit Agricole (Suisse) SA, Geneva
Steve Donzé	Macroeconomist Pictet Asset Management SA, Geneva
Jean-Marc Falter	Advisor Swiss National Bank, Geneva
Gene Frieda	Global Strategist Moore Capital, London
Patrice Gautry	Chief Economist UBP, Geneva
Gaston Gelos	Division Chief Global Financial Stability Analysis IMF, Washington, DC
Hans Genberg	Adviser The SEACEN Centre, Kuala Lumpur
Stefan Gerlach	Deputy Governor Central Bank of Ireland, Dublin
Michel Girardin	Professor of Macrofinance Geneva School of Economics and Management University of Geneva

Charles Goodhart	Professor Emeritus of Banking and Finance London School of Economics
Christos Gortsos	Secretary General Hellenic Bank Association, Athens
Niels Lynggård Hansen	Director and Head of Economics Danmarks Nationalbank, Copenhagen
Harald Hau	Professor of Economics and Finance Geneva School of Economics and Management University of Geneva
Anne Heritier Lachat	President of the Board of Directors FINMA, Bern
Mathias Hoffmann	Professor of International Trade and Finance University of Zürich
Yi Huang	Assistant Professor of Economics Pictet Chair in Finance and Development The Graduate Institute, Geneva
Thomas Huertas	Partner Financial Services Risk Management Ernst & Young LLP (EY), London
Paul Inderbinen	Deputy Head, Multilateral Affairs State Secretariat for International Financial Matters, Basel
Takatoshi Ito	Professor School of International and Public Affairs Columbia University, New York
Thomas Jordan	Chairman of the Governing Board Swiss National Bank, Zürich
Jean Keller	CEO Argos Investment Managers SA, Geneva
Laura Kodres	Assistant Director Institute for Capacity Development IMF, Washington, DC
Randall Kroszner	Professor University of Chicago

Jean-Pierre Landau

Associate Professor and Dean
School of Public Affairs
Sciences Po, Paris

Anne Le Lorier

Deputy Governor
Banque de France, Paris

Valérie Lemaigre

Chief Economist and Head of Investment Office
BCGE, Geneva

Henri Loubergé

Professor of Economics Emeritus
University of Geneva

José Luis Malo de Molina

Director General
Economics, Statistics and Research
Banco de España, Madrid

Tommaso Mancini Griffoli

Monetary Policy
IMF, Washington, DC

Carlo Monticelli

Director General
International Relations
Italian Treasury, Rome

Kiyohiko Nishimura

Dean
Graduate School of Economics
The University of Tokyo

L'udovít Ódor

Council Member
Council for Budget Responsibility, Bratislava

Ugo Panizza

Professor of International Economics
Pictet Chair in Finance and Development
The Graduate Institute, Geneva

Pierre Pâris

CEO
Banque Pâris Bertrand Sturdza, Geneva

Adrien Pichoud

Economist
Global Macro and Fixed Income
Syz Asset Management, Geneva

Charles Pictet

Former Private Banker and Regulator
Pictet & Cie SA, Geneva

Richard Portes

Professor of Economics
London Business School
European University Institute, Florence
CEPR, London

Peter Praet	Member of the Executive Board European Central Bank, Frankfurt
Fabrizio Quirighetti	CIO Global Macro and Fixed Income Syz Bank, Geneva
Jan Fredrik Qvigstad	Executive Director General Staff Central Bank of Norway, Oslo
Lucrezia Reichlin	Professor of Economics London Business School
Luca Ricci	Mission Chief Western Hemisphere Department IMF, Washington, DC
Bertrand Rime	Director Financial Stability Swiss National Bank, Bern
Amlan Roy	Managing Director Global Demographics & Pensions Research Credit Suisse Investment Bank, London
Hans-Joerg Rudloff	Chairman Marcuard Holding Ltd, London
Andrea Siviero	Director Head of International Monetary Cooperation Swiss National Bank, Zürich
Anthony Smouha	CEO Atlanticomnium SA, Geneva
Neal Soss	Vice Chairman Research Credit Suisse, New York
Alexander Swoboda	Professor of Economics Emeritus The Graduate Institute, Geneva
Gianluca Tarolli	Market Economist Research Bordier & Cie, Geneva
Leslie Teo	Chief Economist, Managing Director Economics and Investment Strategy GIC Private Limited, Singapore
Cédric Tille	Professor of Economics The Graduate Institute, Geneva

Albi Tola   Senior Economist
                              International Monetary Relations
                              Swiss National Bank, Zürich

Pascal Towbin   Economist Financial Stability
                              Swiss National Bank, Bern

Edwin Truman   Senior Fellow
                              Peterson Institute for International Economics
                              Washington, DC

Sébastien Waelti   Advisor
                              Office of the Executive Director
                              IMF, Washington, DC

Charles Wyplosz   Professor of International Economics
                              The Graduate Institute, Geneva
                              Director
                              ICMB, Geneva
                              CEPR, London

Geoffrey Yu   Currency Strategist
                              UBS, London

Yongding Yu   Professor
                              Institute of World Economics and Politics, London

Attilio Zanetti   Head of Economic Analysis
                              Swiss National Bank, Zürich

Fritz Zurbruegg   Member of the Governing Board
                              Swiss National Bank. Zürich

Jean Zwahlen   Special Adviser for Asia
                              Union Bancaire Privée, Geneva

Patrick Zweifel   Chief Economist
                              Pictet Asset Management SA, Geneva

Foreword

The 17th Geneva Report on the World Economy follows the series' tradition of providing astute analysis of current economic events in the context of longer-term trends. It reminds us that the trend to lower interest rates originates from far before the Global Crisis of 2008-2009 and takes the view that this process will soon reverse. This view is based on a clear analysis of the factors likely to affect the timescale over which the rebound will occur. The report also draws policy lessons for central banks on the dangers of long-term persistence of low interest rates.

An important aspect is a careful analysis of the integration of China into financial markets and the impact of its returning attention to domestic markets. The report also examines the role of demographic trends and the lessons to be learnt from the deflationary traps that plagued the Japanese economy in the 1990s, and explores unconventional policy instruments that may be deployed to escape such a trap.

The report lays an excellent foundation for further debate of the implications of a decline in the propensity to invest, the factors dictating the speed of the interest rate rebound, and more. It offers a coherent narrative of global economies over the last two decades, marked by the extraordinary event of the Crisis.

CEPR and the ICMB are very grateful to Sir Charles Bean, Christian Broda, Takatoshi Ito and Randall Kroszner for their great efforts in producing this report, and to the participants at the Geneva Conference that took place on 5 May 2015 for their insightful assessments. We are also thankful to Martina Hengge for recording the discussions at the conference, and to Shreya Hewett and Anil Shamdasani for their work in publishing the report.

Charles Wyplosz,   Tessa Ogden
Director, ICMB   Deputy Director, CEPR

September 2015

Executive summary

The past two decades have witnessed an extraordinary decline in both short- and long-term advanced economy interest rates, from levels of around 4-6% to close to zero. Although recent falls have been associated with the financial crisis and its aftermath, the decline in yields, particularly for longer-term rates, began in the late 1990s. Moreover, the fall in yields has been associated primarily with lower real interest rates, rather than a decline in inflation expectations. Finally, the phenomenon has been widespread, and not specific to particular countries.

This report explores the underlying factors behind this decline in global real interest rates and some of the possible consequences, including for policy. While there are several competing explanations, whose effects are not easy to disentangle, our analysis of the evidence suggests that an increase in the propensity to save, driven in particular by demographic developments, is likely to have been an important contributory factor. The integration of China into global financial markets has probably resulted in additional downward pressure on global real interest rates in recent years.

We find less to support the idea that a fall-off in profitable investment opportunities – and thus in the demand for funds to invest – has been a contributory factor over the whole period, though a lower propensity to invest in the wake of the financial crisis is likely to have played some role. Shifts in the preferences of investors towards safe bonds and away from riskier assets, such as equities, also appear to have reinforced the downward pressure on safe interest rates, though here the evidence is somewhat ambiguous.

While the downward trend in rates has been pretty remorseless since the late 1990s, it would be unwise simply to assume that the trend will be maintained. Indeed in many countries, nominal interest rates are already close to their lower bound – in some cases, they are already mildly negative – so further material falls could only come about through higher inflation. But more importantly, some of the forces that have driven real interest rates down are, with time, likely to go into reverse.

In particular, aggregate savings propensities should fall back as the bulge of high-saving middle-aged households moves through into retirement and starts to dissave; this process has already begun. And though Chinese financial integration still has some way to run, the net flow of Chinese savings into global financial markets has already started to ebb as the pattern of Chinese growth rotates towards domestic demand rather than net exports. Finally, the shifts in portfolio preferences may partially unwind as investor confidence slowly returns. But crucially, the time scale over which such a rebound in real interest rates will be manifest is highly uncertain and will be influenced by longer-term fiscal and structural policy choices.

1

Although we believe that there are good reasons to expect real interest rates in due course to recover from their present unusually low levels, it is possible that the present environment will persist for some time yet. So long as it does, there are two particular consequences that will complicate the task of central banks.

First, at least with current inflation targets, episodes where policy rates are constrained by their lower bound are likely to become more frequent and prolonged. Our case study of Japan illustrates how easy it is in such circumstances to slip into a deflationary trap – and how difficult it can be to escape it. Reaching that policy rate lower bound requires the deployment of unconventional monetary policies instead, but the effectiveness of such policies is likely to be subject to diminishing returns. Although there are ways of alleviating the lower bound constraint and restoring scope for the use of conventional interest rate policy, each also carries drawbacks.

Second, and possibly more importantly, a world of persistently low interest rates may be more prone to generating a leveraged 'reach for yield' by investors and speculative asset-price boom-busts. While prudential policies should be the first line of defence against such financial stability risks, their efficacy is by no means assured. In that case, monetary policy may need to come into play as a last line of defence. The bottom line is that the risk-return trade-off facing monetary policymakers is somewhat less favourable than it was. That places added value on the adoption of longer-term fiscal and structural policies that encourage investment and lead to an early recovery in longer-term real interest rates.

1 Introduction

It is almost seven years since the seizure in global financial markets and a sharp recession in the advanced economies, from which recovery has been painfully slow. Central bank policy rates in the main advanced economies remain at, or near, their effective floor. In the Eurozone, Denmark, Sweden and Switzerland, the commercial banks have even been paying to leave funds on deposit with the central bank.

Moreover, the major advanced economy central banks have also adopted unconventional monetary policies – forward guidance and quantitative easing – with the intent of providing additional monetary stimulus by further lowering longer-term interest rates. These have fallen to historically low levels, with negative yields recorded on some of the sovereign debt of several Eurozone members.

This report examines the causes and consequences of this period of unusually low interest rates. We begin by documenting some of the key characteristics of the recent behaviour of interest rates. In particular, the decline in longer-term interest rates began several years before the crisis, suggesting that forces other than the financial crisis were at work driving yields down. Moreover, the fall in yields was primarily accounted for by lower real interest rates rather than a decline in inflation expectations. Finally, it has been a global phenomenon, and not specific to particular countries. We also seek to put recent developments into historical context; by any standard, current experience looks to be highly unusual.

Chapter 2 then discusses some of the hypotheses that have been put forward to explain the decline in interest rates. These fall into three broad categories: an increase in the propensity to save; a reduction in the propensity to invest; and shifts in the demand and supply for different types of asset. We believe the evidence supports the idea that shifts in savings, associated especially with demographics, and Chinese financial integration are likely to have been the dominant factors, particularly in the decade or so before the financial crisis. Following the crisis, however, a decline in the propensity to invest and shifts in asset supplies and demands are likely to have played some role too.

Policy rates in the US and Europe only attained their effective lower bound after the global financial crisis of 2007-2008. By that time, Japan had already spent more than a decade with the policy rate at or near its effective floor. Moreover, the demographic trends that we believe have been instrumental in boosting the global propensity to save since the late 1990s have been more advanced in Japan than elsewhere. Chapter 3 therefore reviews recent Japanese economic history with a view to extracting lessons for the likely consequences of population ageing elsewhere, as well as the appropriate macroeconomic policies to counter a deflationary trap.

Chapter 4 considers the consequences should the low interest rate environment persist. One implication is that, at least with current inflation targets of around 2%, the lower bound on central bank policy rates is more likely to bind, and for longer. We therefore consider ways of alleviating that constraint. Persistently low interest rates may also carry implications for the behaviour of investors and financial institutions. Low interest rates encourage consumers and households to take on more debt, and low returns on safe assets may encourage a leveraged search for yield and increase financial vulnerabilities. So this chapter also examines the scope for these to be contained through prudential policies.

This chapter, and the report itself, concludes by considering the prospect for interest rates in the medium term and beyond. Market participants presently appear to believe that current conditions are likely to persist for many years, though our analysis leads us to think that rates should gradually recover from their present very low levels. Our discussion also considers how government policy choices could affect that path.

1.1   Some key facts

We start by recording some of the basic facts regarding the evolution of short and long nominal interest rates over the past couple of decades. Figure 1.1 shows the evolution of official policy rates for the four major advanced economy central banks (the US Federal Reserve, the Bank of Japan, the European Central Bank and the Bank of England), while Figure 1.2 shows the corresponding implied ten-year nominal spot (i.e. zero coupon) yields on sovereign bonds, with German bunds acting as the benchmark sovereign for the Eurozone. Reflecting the experience of the so-called 'two lost decades', Japanese sovereign yields have been low throughout the period, edging down from around 2% in 1997 to zero today. The downward trend is more marked for the other three jurisdictions, with yields starting at around 6-7% and falling to around 2% for the US and UK and to near zero for Germany. It is particularly notable that the financial crisis and subsequent Great Recession registers as little more than a minor blip on this downward trend; other forces have evidently been at work.

Long-term rates can be thought of in large part as being just the sum of expected future short-term rates. Hence expected future monetary policy rates should be a key determinant of longer-term nominal yields. For all four jurisdictions, the perceived likelihood of sovereign default is extremely low, so any premia that are present in long-term rates will be primarily due to other factors, including risk and term premium. In particular, central bank asset purchases (quantitative easing) may affect both expectations of future settings of policy rates and the levels of these premia.

Figure 1.1   Official policy rates

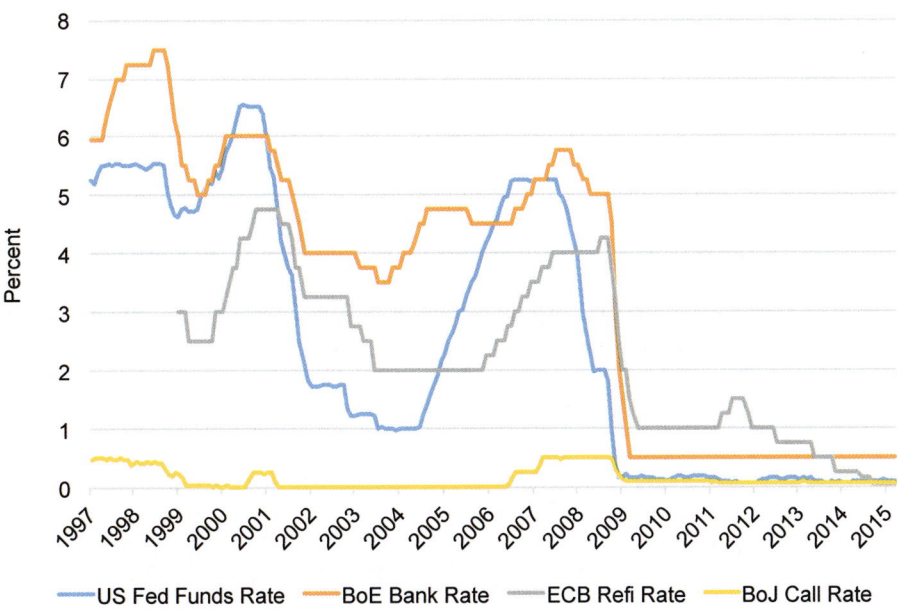

Source: Central bank websites.

Figure 1.2   International ten-year spot yields

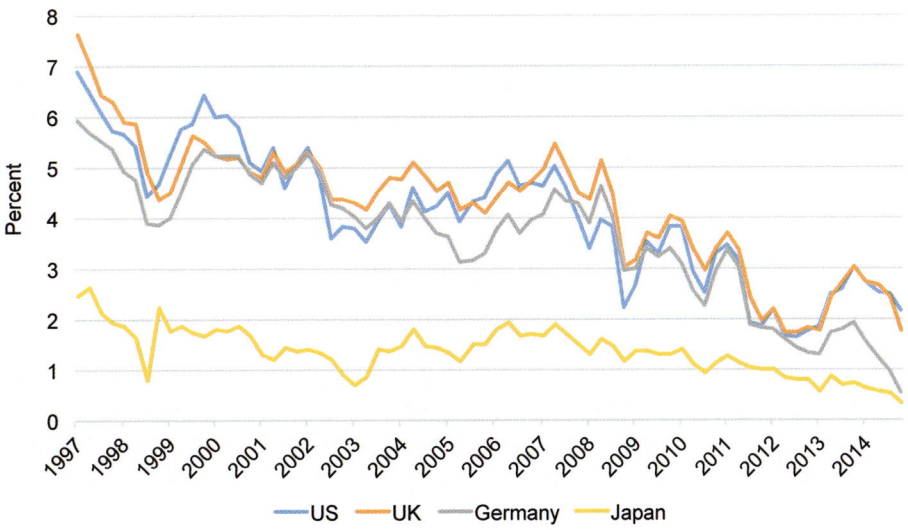

Source: Barclays, Bloomberg mid-yields.

It is important to recognise that future policy settings will in turn reflect the underlying evolution of the economy. Only the Bank of England officially targeted inflation over the whole of the period under consideration, but all four central banks sought to keep inflation low and stable over the medium term, while at the same time accepting temporary fluctuations in inflation associated with cost shocks so as to avoid generating excessive fluctuations in output and employment.

If inflation and inflation expectations are already at their desired rate, and in the absence of cost shocks, keeping inflation on target requires the central bank to set its policy rate so that aggregate demand is equal to the natural (or potential) level of output, i.e. the level of supply that would obtain if wages and prices were fully flexible. The corresponding interest rate is sometimes referred to as the Wicksellian natural rate of interest, after the Swedish economist Knut Wicksell, who introduced the concept more than a century ago; it will be the sum of the natural *real* rate of interest and the inflation target. Were the central bank to choose a lower (higher) rate of interest than the corresponding natural rate, it would generate excess demand (supply) and inflation above (below) the target. And if the central bank were to continue to do that, it could be expected to lead inflation to spiral upwards or downwards.

When inflation starts above (below) target and there is inertia in the inflation process, the central bank will need to choose a policy rate above (below) the natural rate in order to bring inflation and inflation expectations back to the target. But this deviation should only need to last as long as it takes to get inflation back on track. By the same token, when there are cost shocks present, the central bank may conclude that temporary deviations from the natural rate – and temporary deviations of inflation from the target – are warranted in order to avoid the associated fluctuations in activity.

It follows that, if the central bank is seeking to maintain stable inflation, the policy rate should only deviate from its natural level temporarily. To understand the evolution of interest rates over the medium term and beyond, we therefore need to focus on the underlying real forces driving the natural real rate of interest, together with any changes in the inflation objective of the central bank. This view is supported by the empirical work of Stefan Gerlach and Laura Moretti (2014), who find that movements in central bank policy rates have primarily been a response to the underlying economic forces driving down real rates, rather than reducing them independently (see also Justiniano and Primiceri, 2010). Moreover, our interest is in the persistent trends rather than short-term fluctuations. For that reason, it is natural to focus more on the evolution of long-term, rather than short-term, interest rates.

In order to dig deeper into the reasons for lower long-term rates – a task for Chapter 2 – we decompose the movements in the nominal long-term yield into those movements that are associated with changes in expected inflation, and which might therefore simply represent changes in the perceived inflation objective, and those that are associated with changes in the real long-term natural rate of interest. Fortunately, the increased issuance of indexed sovereign debt in recent years facilitates the derivation of reasonably convincing proxies for the expected inflation component in a way for the period in question. It is, though, inevitably a more contentious exercise for earlier periods when observable proxies are unavailable.

The left-hand panel of Figure 1.3 shows the ten-year spot yield on US Treasury inflation-protected securities (TIPS, first issued in 1997) alongside the corresponding ten-year spot nominal yield. The former therefore provides a direct measure of the ten-year real interest rate for the US, while the difference between the two series provides a measure of average expected inflation over the following ten years. The right-hand panel shows equivalent series for the UK, where indexed gilts (IG) were first issued back in 1987. It is apparent that the decline in nominal yields is almost entirely a consequence of a decline in real yields. The difference between the real and nominal yields – implied inflation expectations – has been remarkably stable, reflecting the successful anchoring of inflation expectations under the inflation-targeting regime that was adopted in the UK in 1992.

Figure 1.3   Decomposition of nominal ten-year yields

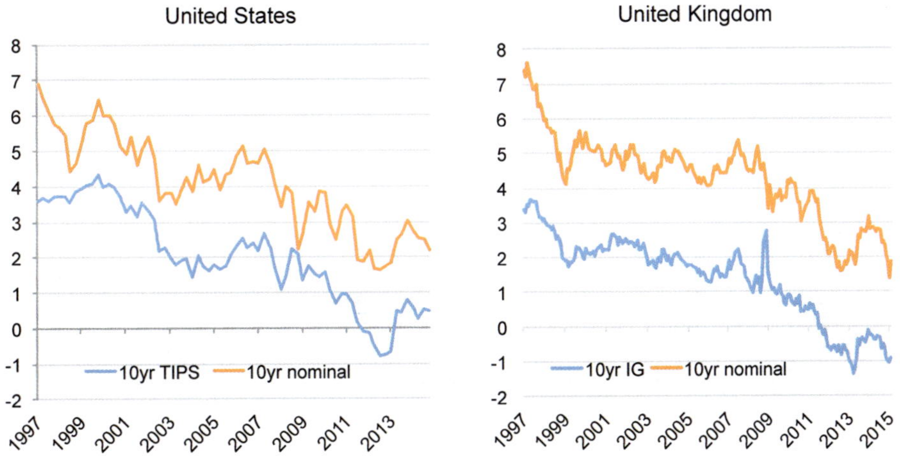

Source: Barclays, Bloomberg mid-yields and Bank of England.

While nominal yields may differ significantly across countries because of different inflation trends, real yields should move quite closely together if the constituent financial markets are well integrated and default risk is not a major issue. There may be some differences in so far as the national real interest rates are measured with respect to different baskets of prices. In particular, any trends in real exchange rates are likely to be associated with cross-country differences in real interest rates. However, these seem likely to be relatively modest and short-lived, particularly when comparing countries at similar stages of development. In that case, we can meaningfully talk about a single 'world' real interest rate.

In Figure 1.4, we follow the approach of Mervyn King and David Low (2014) by averaging across the ten-year real yields on the sovereign debt of the G7 countries, excluding Italy, in order to obtain a measure of the corresponding 'world' risk-free real interest rate. The sample of countries is necessarily unbalanced, as the number of countries issuing indexed debt grows over time. At the beginning, the measure relies exclusively on UK debt, with other countries being added as time progresses. King and Low calculate both an unweighted arithmetic average and a measure weighted by country size and find the measures are very similar, except for a short period around 1998-1999 immediately after the introduction of US TIPS. We therefore just present a simple unweighted measure.

Figure 1.4   'World' ten-year risk-free real interest rate

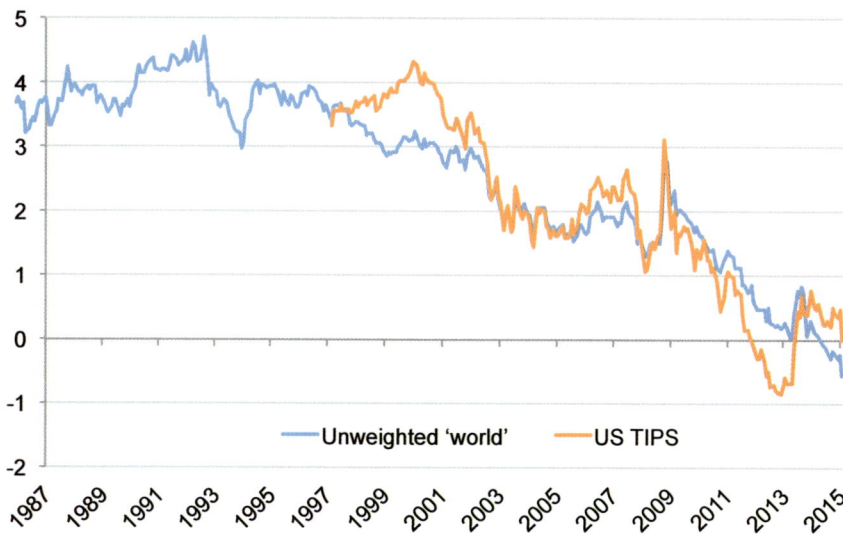

Notes: 'World' real interest rate is an unbalanced simple average of G7 ex Italy ten-year real yields. Sliced UK indexed gilts were used to proxy world real yields from 1985-1996. From 1997-2006, 'World' rates were calculated using a simple average of spliced US ten-year TIPS and UK IGs. From 2007-2008, 'World' rates were calculated using a simple average of spliced ten-year US, UK, Canada, Japan, and France indexed bonds. From 2008-2015, 'World' rates were calculated using a simple average of spliced 10-year US, UK, Canada, Japan, France, and Germany.

Source: Barclays, Bloomberg mid yields.

Unsurprisingly, Figure 1.4 simply reinforces the message from Figure 1.3: the world long-term real risk-free rate has been drifting down remorselessly from around 4% in the late 1990s to just below zero today. This figure also plots the US real yield separately. Aside from the 1998-1999 discrepancy, US yields are noticeably lower than those elsewhere – by around 50-100 basis points – during the 2009-2013 period. This almost surely reflects a 'safe haven' demand for US sovereign bonds in the aftermath of the financial crisis, together with the impact of the US Federal Reserve's programme of asset purchases. But this discount has now disappeared; indeed, US yields are slightly higher than elsewhere.

We conclude this quick tour of the facts with a look at developments in a sample of emerging economies. Most of these countries do not issue indexed sovereign debt. Moreover, inflation rates differ across countries and over time. We are therefore forced to employ nominal yields and then attempt to adjust for inflation differences. In principle, one could attempt to derive regression-based measures of projected inflation a decade ahead. But we simply assume that current inflation provides a reasonable guide to expected future inflation and subtract annual inflation from the nominal bond yield in order to construct a real interest rate measure.

This measure is shown in Figure 1.5. As default (and exchange-rate) risk is often material for these countries, we would expect it to exceed the (risk-free) rate for the advanced economies shown in Figure 1.4. Moreover, this premium can be expected to vary with perceptions of default risk. The figure suggests that emerging economy real rates have also been falling since the late 1990s. The premium above the advanced economy ('world') rate is large during 1998-2001, following the Asian financial crisis, but falls back to very low levels immediately prior to the 2007-2008 financial crisis. But, in contrast to the continued decline seen in the advanced economies, emerging economy real rates seem to have been relatively stable since then. The corollary of that would be a rise in the corresponding risk premium. This is an issue we return to in Chapter 2.

Figure 1.5   Emerging economies ten-year real interest rate

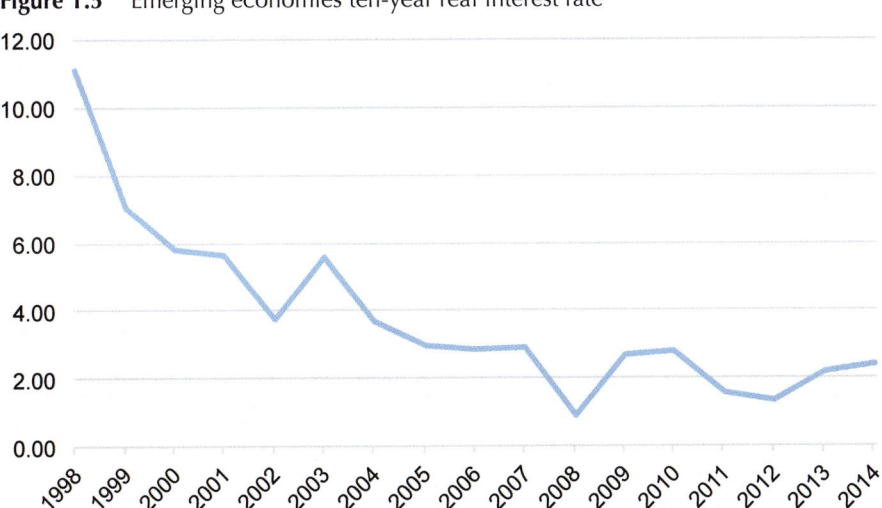

Notes: Unbalanced arithmetic average of 12 emerging economies' ten-year government bond yields less annual inflation. Sample: 1998 Phillippines; 1999 add Malaysia, Poland, South Africa; 2000 add Thailand; 2001 add South Korea; 2002-2006 add Colombia, Israel, India; 2007-2009 add Brazil; 2010 add Turkey; 2011-2014 add Mexico.

1.2   Historical context

How unusual are the recent developments in interest rates from a historical perspective? We start by examining the post-war period, where data for a wide range of countries are available. Even so, consistent series for longer-term yields are only available for a few countries, so we focus instead on the behaviour of shorter-term rates. Figure 1.6 displays two series for the average ex post real return on Treasury bills for groups of advanced and emerging economies, respectively, drawn from the work of Carmen Reinhart and Belen Sbrancia (2015).

Figure 1.6   Average real Treasury-bill rates, 1946-2014

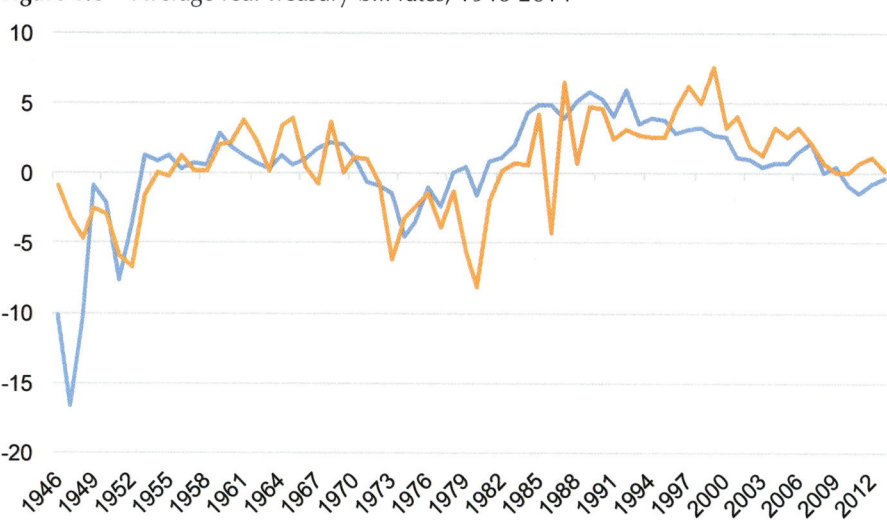

Notes: Advanced economies are: Australia, Belgium, Canada, France, Germany, Greece, Ireland, Italy, Japan, New Zealand, Sweden, United States, and United Kingdom. Emerging economies are: Brazil, Egypt, India, Korea, Malaysia, Mexico, Philippines, South Africa, Turkey and Venezuela.

Source: Reinhart and Sbrancia (2014).

At first glance, the figure suggests that recent experience is not particularly unusual. Indeed, real interest rates were below those seen today both for the decade after the conclusion of World War II and then again during the 1970s. Moreover, rates, though positive, remained relatively low even during the intervening decade and a half from 1955 to 1969. In many respects, however, this was an atypical period. During the first part of the period, market interest rates were often subject to regulatory caps and regulatory requirements, and limited international capital mobility meant a large captive domestic audience for government debt. In short, it was a period of so-called 'financial repression' in which observed rates of return were kept significantly below the level that would have obtained in an unrestricted environment. And the 1970s were, of course, a time of unexpectedly high inflation. Reinhart and Sbrancia provide a rich discussion of the period and the part played by financial repression in alleviating the post-war public debt burdens facing many of the combatants.

In contrast to the first half of the post-war period, the recent period of falling real interest rates has been associated neither with financial repression nor unexpectedly high inflation. Until the post-crisis re-regulation of the banking sector, the trend was entirely in the direction of reducing the constraints on financial institutions, while inflation was extremely stable during the Great Moderation period that preceded the financial crisis and, if anything, has tended to be lower than expected since the crisis. Given the rather different circumstances that prevailed during the first half of the post-war period, it therefore seems inappropriate to view recent experience as just a return to post-war norms, following a 1980s interregnum of higher returns driven by higher inflation risk premia.

What about earlier historical experience? A recent study by James Hamilton, Ethan Harris, Jan Hatzius and Ken West (2015) provides some useful analysis of the behaviour of short-term ex ante real interest rates for 17 countries going back as far as the beginning of the early nineteenth century. They first estimate simple time-varying auto-regressive models of inflation, which are then used to generate one-year-ahead projections for inflation. These are then subtracted from a measure of short-term nominal interest rates to provide time series for expected short-term real interest rates in each country.

These short-term rates will have been influenced by cyclical factors, as well as more slowly evolving structural factors of the sort that dominate our discussion in Chapter 2. In order to abstract from such transient effects, as well as allowing for a time-varying underlying real interest rate, Hamilton and his co-authors estimate first-order auto-regressions for each country's real interest rate on a rolling 30-year sample. For each sample estimate, they then obtain an estimate of the associated long-run steady state. These are then averaged across countries to provide a time-varying series for the 'world' long-run real interest rate, shown in Figure 1.7, together with their series for the US short-term ex ante real interest rate. In line with Reinhart and Sbrancia, their estimates suggest that the only analogue to recent experience is the period around and immediately after World War II.

Figure 1.7   Estimates of US short-term and long-run 'world' real interest rates

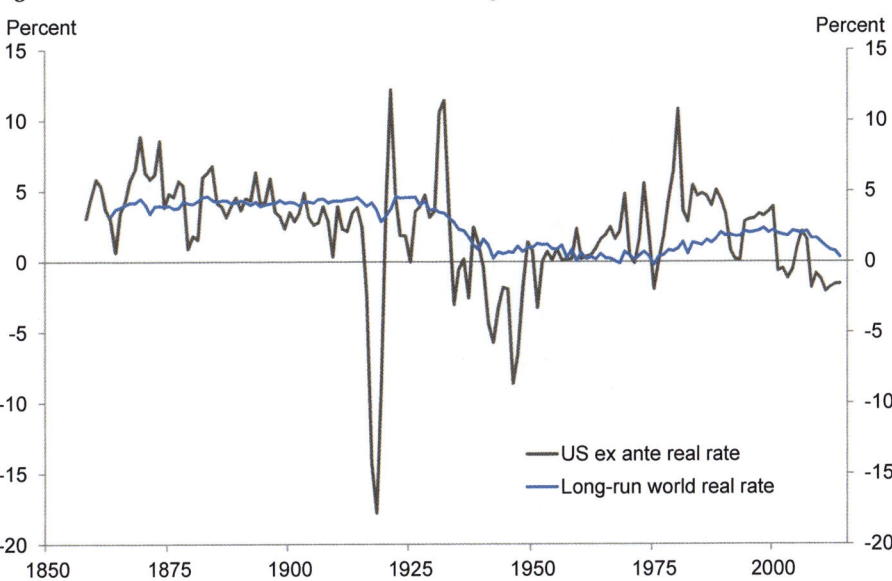

Source: Hamilton et al. (2015).

To conclude this review of historical experience, we complement the analyses of Reinhart and Sbrancia and Hamilton et al. by providing some new estimates of long-term real interest rates in the UK that go even further back in time – to the beginning of the eighteenth century. Focusing on the UK makes sense, as the international financial system was relatively open and integrated during the nineteenth and early twentieth centuries, with London very much standing at its centre. Consequently, the evolution of the UK long-term real interest rate can be expected to provide a decent proxy for the behaviour of the 'world' real interest rate. Moreover, not only are long runs of back data available for the UK, but it is also one of the few countries for which a long-term nominal interest rate on government debt is available on a consistent basis throughout the period, in this case the yield on 2.5% consols. We can therefore utilise a direct measure of long-term yields, rather than making inferences about the long term from regression equations as in the study by Hamilton et al.

In order to construct an expected real counterpart to the consol rate, we first need to construct an appropriate measure of expected inflation. As a consol is a perpetuity, the relevant measure of expected inflation is a present value of expected inflation at all future dates. We construct this present value by first estimating auxiliary vector autoregressions in inflation and the consol yield and then using the results to generate inflation projections for multiple years ahead. For the Gold Standard period, up until 1931, we assume a stable inflationary process, though we allow for temporary deviations during and immediately after major wars when convertibility into gold was temporarily suspended. For the fiat money period after 1931, we allow the inflation process to evolve, corresponding to the successive changes in monetary regime during this latter period. An annex to this chapter provides more detail on the estimation approach and the evaluation of the appropriately weighted measure of expected future inflation.

Although the data suggest that inflation was quite volatile from year to year in the eighteenth and nineteenth centuries,[1] the Gold Standard imparted a high degree of long-run stability to prices. As a consequence, our estimates of expected inflation during that period are relatively insensitive to precisely how we model inflation. Under the subsequent fiat money standard, however, inflation is a much less stable process, meaning that the estimates of the real consol rate for the post-1931 period are correspondingly less reliable.

Figure 1.8 shows our series for the nominal and expected real consol yields. Recent nominal yields do not quite match the previous historic lows seen after World War II and before that in the late nineteenth century, but they are still pretty low compared to recent experience. Reflecting the stability in price expectations imparted by the Gold Standard, the nominal and real yields are very close until 1931, with just small deviations during periods when convertibility was suspended.

---

1   This probably reflects both greater measurement error in the historical data and genuine volatility due to the vagaries of harvests, etc.

Figure 1.8   300 years of UK nominal and real long-term yields

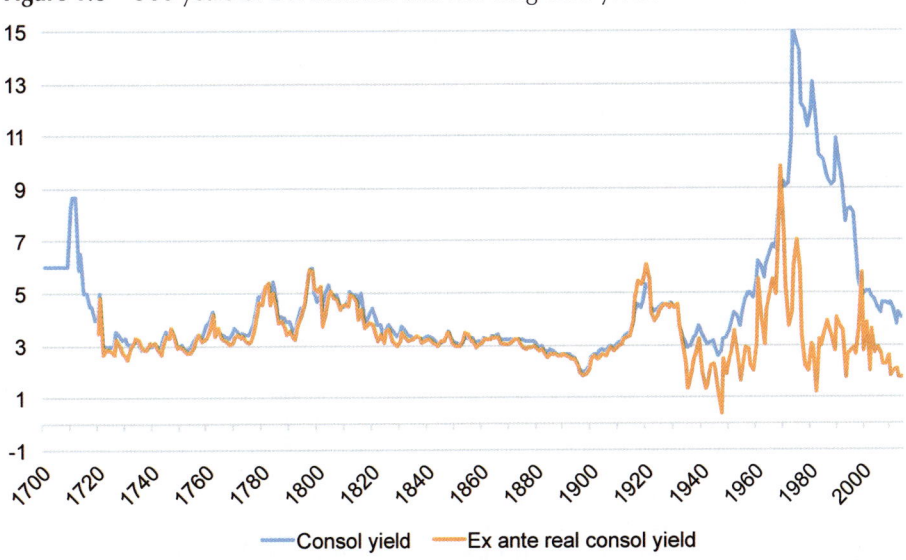

Source: Bank of England Historical database (http://www.bankofengland.co.uk/research/Pages/onebank/datasets.aspx#4) and own calculations.

After 1931, during the fiat money period, the expected inflation measure is higher, so that the divergence between the two yield series becomes more pronounced. The expected inflation measure also fluctuates much more from year to year, reflecting the difficulty in capturing the changes in the inflation process properly. For that reason, it is more sensible to focus on the broad movements over this period, rather than short-lived spikes up or down. The picture is broadly similar to that obtained by Reinhart and Sbrancia and by Hamilton et al., though the period of low real rates during and after World War II is somewhat more short-lived than in their estimates. In any case, the only precedent for the current low level of real long-term interest rates seems to be this rather idiosyncratic episode, characterised by the combination of financial repression and elevated inflation. In contrast, the recent decline took place in deregulated financial markets when inflation was generally low and stable.

1.3   Summary

We may summarise the key findings of this chapter as follows:

- Short-term nominal interest rates in the advanced economies – excluding Japan, where they were already very low – fell sharply after the 2007-2008 financial crisis and have remained at or near their effective lower bound since. But the decline in long-term risk-free nominal interest rates – again excluding Japan – is not simply a consequence of the financial crisis; these rates have been falling steadily since the late 1990s.

- This fall in long-term nominal rates reflects a steady decline over two decades in the long-term risk-free real interest rate, rather than a fall in expected inflation, which has remained broadly stable.
- Long-term real interest rates have also fallen in the emerging economies, though this fall seems to have halted around the time of the financial crisis. These rates are more open to default risk.

The very low level of long-term risk-free real interest rates in the advanced economies is historically most unusual. Real rates have rarely been so low; when they have been, it has almost invariably been during or after a war, when there was a degree of financial repression and/or inflation was elevated. The present configuration of low real rates with low inflation appears to be unprecedented.

Chapter 1 Annex: Expected inflation and the UK real consol yield

In order to derive a historical series for the real yield on UK consols, we first need to derive a measure of expected inflation. To do this, we rely on projections of future inflation generated from simple vector autoregressions (VAR) in the inflation rate and the nominal yield on 2.5% consols; two lags of each endogenous variable are included. As the consol rate should respond to changes in expected inflation, it potentially provides useful information about expected future movements in inflation. We also experimented with a larger system including GDP growth, but found that it added little additional statistical explanatory power.

The data for the exercise are taken from the Bank of England historical database (available at http://www.bankofengland.co.uk/research/Pages/onebank/datasets.aspx#4). The price index used to calculate inflation is the implied GDP deflator at market prices. We use this measure in preference to the alternative series based on consumer prices because the volatility of the latter before 1870 is significantly greater. Before 1870, the basic data underlying the price series are less comprehensive and reliable. While it is plausible that the overall price index was somewhat more variable in the eighteenth and early nineteenth centuries, when agricultural goods constituted a much larger share of the consumption basket, the very high volatility and negative serial correlation in the consumer price inflation series also suggests that measurement error is rather greater than for the less volatile deflator series.

We adopt two different approaches to estimating the VAR: one for the pre-1931 period when monetary policy was governed by a commodity (gold) standard; and another for the subsequent period of fiat money when the monetary regime was repeatedly changing. For the pre-1931 period, we assume the inflation process is fixed. Starting in 1720, we recursively estimate the coefficients of the VAR, period by period and using all available past data. We then use the results of each estimation to generate forecasts of future inflation corresponding to each sample for several periods ahead.

There are two periods that warrant special treatment: the Revolutionary and Napoleonic Wars (1792-1815); and the Great War (1914-18). In both cases, convertibility into gold was suspended for all, or a large part of, the conflict, allowing monetary finance to take place. After the wars were concluded, in each case there followed a period of constriction as the country prepared for a return to gold at the old parity in 1821 and 1925, respectively. We therefore allow for intercept shifts during wartime and subsequent intercept shifts during the post-war periods leading up to the re-adoption of a commodity standard. When it comes to projecting inflation during these periods, we (somewhat arbitrarily) assume that private agents believe the period of war/constriction will continue for just one more year.

Our approach to the period after the UK left gold in 1931 is a little different. The period from then until now has been characterised by a series of different monetary regimes, including: benign neglect/pure discretion; fixed but adjustable exchange rates under the Bretton Woods system; monetary targeting; shadowing the Deutsche mark; and inflation targeting. It therefore does not make sense to assume a fixed inflation process. Instead, we allow it to evolve by estimating a series of 25-year long rolling regressions (i.e. a moving sample window rather than an ever expanding one, as was the case before 1931), which are then used to generate the forecasts for future inflation. We also include an intercept shift dummy for World War II and dummies for the 1973 and 1979 oil price shocks.

In order to use the expected inflation series to construct a real consol yield, we first need to allow for the fact that a consol is a perpetuity paying a constant coupon indefinitely, rather than a pure discount bond delivering no coupon and just a payment at the terminal date. The data for longer-term interest rates covering the recent past in this report generally focus on the synthetic yield on such a pure discount bond derived from the market prices of a range of actual coupon-carrying bonds. Unfortunately, the range of bonds issued over the whole period is not wide enough to allow a similar approach to constructing historical yield data back to the early 1700s.

A perpetuity is, however, equivalent to a sequence of pure discount bonds. Using the Campbell-Shiller linearisation and ignoring risk premia, we can write the nominal yield, i_t^∞, on a perpetuity as:

$$i_t^\infty = (1 - \rho) \sum_{j=0}^{j=\infty} \rho^j i_{t+j}$$

where $\rho \equiv 1/(1 + i_t^\infty)$ and $\{i_t, i_{t+1}, i_{t+2}, ...\}$ is the sequence of current and (expected) future one-period spot yields. This expression says that the yield is just a weighted average of current and future expected one-period spot yields, where the weights decline geometrically.

Finally, we use the Fisher equation to write:

$$(1 + r) = (1 + i)/(1 + \pi) \Rightarrow r \approx i - \pi$$

where r is the real rate corresponding to the nominal rate i and π is the corresponding (expected) inflation rate. Hence we can define a real rate on the perpetuity as:

$$r_t^\infty = (1 - \rho) \sum_{j=0}^{j=\infty} \rho^j r_{t+j}$$

$$= (1 - \rho) \sum_{j=0}^{j=\infty} \rho^j (i_{t+j} - \pi_{t+j})$$

$$= i_t^\infty - (1 - \rho) \sum_{j=0}^{j=\infty} \rho^j \pi_{t+j}$$

$$\approx i_t^\infty - \frac{(1 - \rho)}{(1 - \rho^n)} \sum_{j=0}^{j=n-1} \rho^j \pi_{t+j}$$

The penultimate line therefore just gives the real yield on the perpetuity as the nominal yield less a suitably weighted average of expected future inflation, where the weights again decline geometrically. The final line above just truncates this infinite sum in expected future inflation and is useful for the actual calculations. In practice, we employ expected inflation calculated from the VAR estimates for up to 20 years ahead.

2 Why have (safe) real interest rates fallen?

We now consider the forces behind the decline in interest rates. There is, of course, nothing puzzling in the behaviour of short-term nominal rates, with central banks responding aggressively to the fall in aggregate demand prompted by the 2007-2008 financial crisis. Rather, the puzzle lies in the downward trend in the long-term risk-free real rate that starts well before the crisis. Indeed, ahead of the crisis Federal Reserve Chairman Alan Greenspan famously labelled it a "conundrum" (Greenspan, 2005), which Ben Bernanke shortly afterwards attributed to a "savings glut" in China in particular (Bernanke, 2005). There are, however, several possible explanations as to why the propensity to save might have risen. Moreover, any decline in the propensity to invest could also be expected to place downward pressure on the natural real interest rate. And changes in the relative demands for, and supplies of, risk-free and risky assets may also have played a role.

This chapter discusses some of the competing hypotheses and their congruence with the facts. As we noted in Chapter 1, although the main proximate determinant of long-term interest rates is expectations of future short-term interest rates, in normal times we would expect the central bank to ensure the interest rate is at its natural level, consistent with achieving full employment (except if inflation expectations are not at the right level to begin with or in the presence of cost shocks). So the primary focus of the discussion needs to be on the real economic factors that have pushed this rate lower since the late 1990s.

Initially, we frame the discussion in terms of a simple loanable funds diagram, shown in Figure 2.1, though we extend this apparatus later. The figure is drawn making the conventional assumption that substitution effects associated with changes in the interest rate dominate income effects, so that savings (SS) is increasing in 'the' real interest rate, while investment (II) is a decreasing function of the real interest rate. Initially, both of these relationships are drawn assuming that output is at potential. The figure suggests that the observed fall in real interest rates is potentially attributable either to an exogenous fall in the propensity to invest (i.e. a leftward shift in the II schedule, taking the economy from O to O_I) or an exogenous increase in the propensity to save (i.e. a rightward shift in the SS schedule, taking the economy from O to O_S), or to some combination of both.

Figure 2.1   Global market for loanable funds

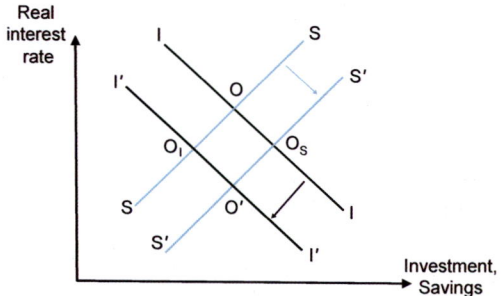

This conceptual framework seems quite adequate for the decade or so of the Great Moderation that led up to the financial crisis and Great Recession. During that period, inflation was low and stable, cost shocks were small, unemployment was low and nominal interest rates were well above zero. So interest rates were likely to be close to their natural level. Matters are, though, more complex after 2009. Since then, many advanced economy central banks have operated with policy rates at, or close to, their zero lower bound, and therefore potentially above the level of the natural rate of interest.

How does this affect the framework? Suppose first that other policies – for instance, fiscal policy or unconventional monetary policies – are successfully deployed to maintain full employment. This corresponds to the generation of endogenous movements in the SS and II schedules so as to bring the natural rate of interest up to the level consistent with policy rates being at their effective lower bound.

In practice, although fiscal policy turned highly expansionary in 2009-2010 and central banks became increasingly aggressive in their deployment of unconventional monetary tools such as large-scale asset purchases (quantitative easing), full employment was not maintained, leaving those economies operating with output below potential and substantial underutilised resources. As far as the diagram is concerned, that shortfall in activity below potential is likely to be associated with a lower volume of savings (shifting SS to the left) and possibly lower investment too (also shifting II to the left). In any case, it is activity, rather than the interest rate, which must adjust to keep the demand and supply of funds in line with each other when the policy is constrained by its lower bound.

Consequently, the (unobserved) natural interest rate will have been below the rate actually observed in the financial markets. Since 2009, recorded interest rates probably overstate the natural rate of interest, which will have been even lower. The gap between the observed and the natural rates of interest will, though, have been declining in recent times as the recovery has strengthened and unemployment has fallen back towards more normal rates. Our case study of Japan in Chapter 3 expands further on how reaching the zero lower bound on policy rates alters the dynamic behaviour of an economy.

Higher savings or lower investment? An identification challenge

Figure 2.1 suggests that the evolution of the overall quantity of savings and investment could help to identify whether a higher propensity to save or a lower propensity to invest has been more important in driving interest rates lower since the late 1990s. If overall savings and investment have risen, it would seem natural to attribute the fall in real interest rates primarily to a rise in the propensity to save. Conversely, if overall savings and investment have fallen, it would seem natural to attribute the fall in real interest rates primarily to a decline in the propensity to invest.

Figure 2.2 shows the savings (dashed lines) and investment (solid lines) shares for the world as a whole (in red), as well as for the advanced economies (in green) and the emerging and developing economies (in blue) separately, with the gap between savings and investment corresponding to the trade surplus/deficit.[2] The most striking feature is the sharp increase in savings and investment shares in the emerging and developing economies that begins in the late 1990s. Moreover, savings runs ahead of investment, primarily reflecting the Chinese trade surplus. This rise in the savings and investment shares of the emerging and developed economies is mirrored by a decline in their advanced economy counterparts – especially so in 2009. As a consequence, the global savings/investment share turns out to have been remarkably stable over the period as a whole – if anything, there is just a hint of an upward trend – with the only major (downward) movement coming during the Great Recession.

Figure 2.2   Savings and investment shares (% of GDP)

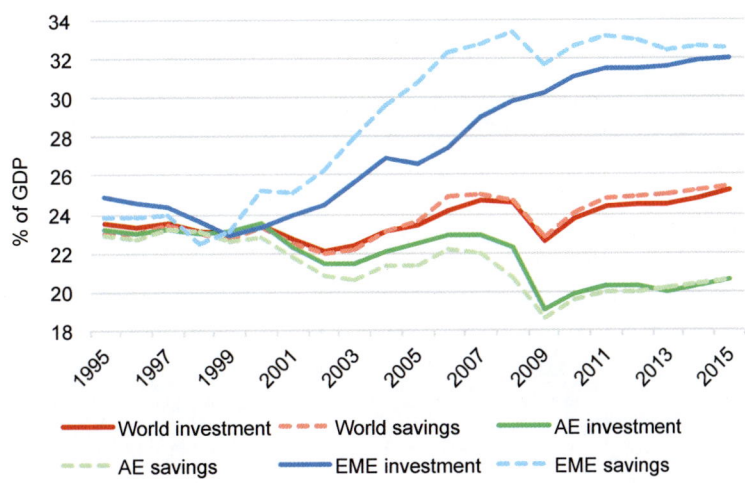

Source: IMF WEO database.

---

2   Since global savings must in theory equal global investment, the small excess of global savings over global investment in the data must reflect measurement error.

This broad stability in global savings/investment has led some commentators to conclude that a savings glut of the sort identified by Bernanke cannot be the primary explanation for the decline in real interest rates (e.g. Eichengreen, 2014). But that same argument could equally well be deployed to infer that a fall in the propensity to invest cannot explain the decline in interest rates, other than around the time of the Great Recession.

Of course, Figure 2.1 already hints at one possible solution to this conundrum: there could have been a *simultaneous* rise in the overall propensity to save and a decline in the overall propensity to invest, such that the world economy has gradually moved vertically downwards from O to O' over the past 15 years or so. This *might* be the answer, but it seems like a little bit too much of a coincidence that these two forces have balanced each other out in terms of their net impact on global savings/investment, especially given the length of the period in question.

Such a fortuitous combination of events is not, however, the only possible explanation: as the left-hand (right-hand) panel of Figure 2.3 shows, if savings (investment) is insensitive to movements in the interest rate so that SS (II) is close to being vertical, then a fall (rise) in the propensity to invest (save) will result in a fall in the interest rate without any associated change in quantities. So an alternative explanation for the broad stability of the global savings/investment share is that savings (investment) is relatively insensitive to changes in interest rates and that most of the variation in interest rates is the result of changes in the propensity to invest (save). Moreover, the fact that there *is* one period in particular when there is a marked (positive) correlation between movements in real interest rates and the global savings/investment share – the Great Recession, when both fall – suggests that it is more likely to be investment that is relatively insensitive to interest rate movements rather than savings.

Figure 2.3 Implications of interest insensitivity

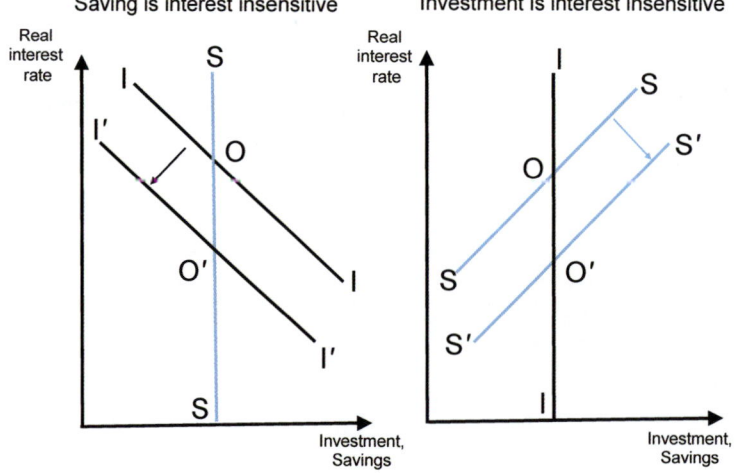

Investment, Savings

Consequently, while we cannot rely on the evolution of the global savings/investment share to identify the drivers of the decline in interest rates, we can still look directly at the correlation between those drivers and the movements in interest rates. In particular, we need to find factors that shifted in the right direction at the same time as long-term real rates started falling in the late 1990s; timing is everything, in other words. From Figure 2.2, one obvious candidate is the rise in the savings rate in the emerging and developing economies. But it is by no means the only possible explanation. The rest of this chapter therefore looks at possible explanations and whether they pass the timing test.

Box 2.1   Secular stagnation

The confluence of falling long-term real interest rates and slow output growth since the financial crisis has led several authors – most notably, Robert Gordon (2012, 2014) and Larry Summers (2013) – to suggest that the US, and the advanced economies more generally, may have entered a period of 'secular stagnation'. This revives a hypothesis originally developed by Alvin Hansen in his 1938 Presidential Address to the American Economic Association (Hansen, 1939). In this address, Hansen pointed to a fall-off in investment opportunities in the US driven by slowing population growth, the end of opportunities created by territorial expansion to the West, and a decline in the rate of innovation. As a consequence there was, he argued, a chronic tendency for an excess supply of savings to open up and, with it, a tendency for insufficient aggregate demand.

Gordon's arguments are similar to those of Hansen, though his case rests in large part on the idea that the rapid growth of the past 250 years since the start of the Industrial Revolution has been on the back of three unique sets of innovations: the steam engine and the railroads; electricity and the internal combustion engine; and the digital revolution. But Gordon is doubtful that the future will bring more such fundamental advances. Accordingly, he suggests, the rate of total factor productivity growth will fall back to the much slower rates that obtained in earlier human history. Moreover, reduced fertility and less immigration mean that the rate of growth of the labour force in these countries – and with it the amount of additional capital needed – is also slowing. Both these factors mean the rate of growth of potential output will be lower, as well as placing downward pressure on the equilibrium interest rate.

Summers' argument is more Keynesian in spirit. His argument rests on the idea that shifts in the propensity to save and invest – of the sort we discuss in the main text of this report – have driven the natural or Wicksellian (nominal) rate of interest consistent with full employment to below zero. As a result, because of the zero lower bound on policy rates – and in the absence of sufficiently aggressive countervailing fiscal policy – there will be an endemic tendency for labour and capital to be underutilised. Moreover, if that underutilisation feeds back into lower investment in physical and human capital through hysteresis effects, then it may also adversely affect growth in potential output. Weak demand thus begets weak supply, rather than the other way round (as in Gordon's story).

While the main text employs a simple, and somewhat eclectic, loanable funds framework for analysing the impact of the various forces affecting the equilibrium interest rate, it is useful here to consider a widely used, though rather more tightly drawn, theoretical apparatus that directly connects the growth rate to the real interest rate. In particular, suppose that households can borrow and lend freely at the (known) real rate of interest r_t and that within-period utility takes the form (ignoring labour supply, for simplicity): $U(C) = C^{1-\alpha}/(1 - \alpha)$. At each point in time, households plan a path for consumption that will maximise the value of their lifetime utility, subject to the resources available to them over their lives. It is well known that the associated intertemporal optimality condition then takes the form:

$$E_t[\Delta c_{t+1}] = (r_t + \alpha^2\sigma^2/2 - \delta)/\alpha$$

where c_t is the logarithm of consumption at date t, δ is the household discount rate, σ^2 is the variance of the growth rate of consumption, $E_t[.]$ denotes the conditional expectation at t, and Δ denotes a first difference (so Δc_{t+1} is the growth rate of consumption between t and $t + 1$). Hence, under these assumptions, there should be a tight relationship between the expected rate of growth of consumption and the real interest rate. Moreover, because consumption growth and output growth are highly correlated, this relationship also points to a positive correlation between expected output growth and the real interest rate.

Unfortunately, despite its widespread use in modern macroeconomic analysis, the empirical performance of this equation leaves something to be desired. For instance, consumption is both excessively responsive to predictable movements in income and excessively smooth, which is typically attributed either to imperfections in credit markets or to myopia. Moreover, the cross-country historical study by Hamilton et al., mentioned in Chapter 1, finds only a very weak statistical relationship between historical variations in real interest rates and the growth rate of output.

Notwithstanding this, Figure 2.A presents a little bit of evidence against the hypothesis that the decline in real rates is the result of a decline in expected output growth. This shows expected US output growth over the coming four quarters, taken from the Survey of Professional Forecasters, together with US long-term real interest rates, measured from TIPS after 1997 and using an ex post measure before that date. This shows that real GDP forecasts have remained roughly unchanged since the early 1990s, other than during the worst of the financial crisis, despite the fall in real interest rates. That contrasts with the widespread perception that real rates and real growth have fallen together. Actual growth may have been weak since the crisis, but this evidence suggests it has not been *expected* to be weak, which is what matters for the story. While this analysis is by no means definitive, we will focus on other factors besides the expected growth rate when trying to understand the drivers of the decline in real interest rates.

Figure 2.A US expected output growth and real interest rates

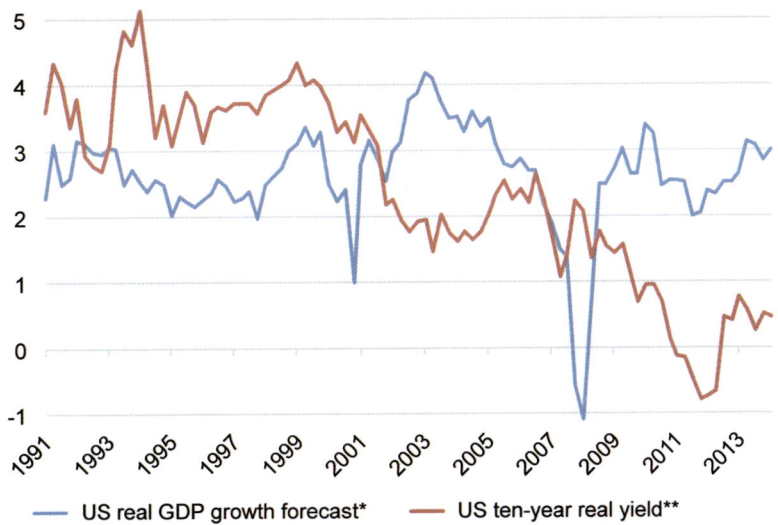

Notes: *Forecast for four-quarter ahead real GDP growth from the Survey of Professional Forecasters.
**Nominal 10-year yield less CPI inflation until 1997; 10-year yield from TIPS thereafter.

Finally, while the discussion in the main text encompasses several of the factors that Summers identifies in his resurrection of the secular stagnation hypothesis, it is worth pointing out that, although secular stagnation may accompany low interest rates, it is by no means necessary. As soon as one departs from the simple consumption framework above, real interest rates can, in principle, be unusually low, even though growth rates remain close to historical norms.

2.1   A higher propensity to save

Beginning with the savings side of the market for funds, there are several reasons why the global propensity to save may have risen.

Demography

Increased longevity and declining fertility mean that populations are ageing almost everywhere. That is especially so in the advanced economies, but is also the case in China and some other emerging economies. These demographic changes potentially affect both individual savings rates and aggregate savings by changing population composition.

First, advances in medical science together with higher living standards in developing and emerging economies mean that people are, on average, living longer almost everywhere. By itself, that need not imply higher savings rates if the increased longevity is matched by later retirement. But that has not generally been the case. According to the OECD (2011), the average state retirement age for men in the OECD countries in 1971 was 63.8 years, while by 2010 it had actually fallen a touch to 62.9 years and on extant plans, was only expected to rise to 64.5 years by 2050 (see Table 2.1). For women, the corresponding figures were 61.9, 61.8 and 64.4 years. But expected life after retirement far outstrips that increase in retirement ages, rising by around seven years between 1971 and 2050.

Table 2.1 Retirement age for males and expected life after retirement

	Retirement age (years)			Life expectancy after retirement (years)		
	1971	2010	2050	1971	2010	2050
Germany	63	65	65	14.1	17.0	20.3
Japan	60	64	65	16.6	19.8	21.6
UK	65	65	68	12.3	16.9	16.9
US	65	66	67	13.2	16.8	17.7
OECD average	63.8	62.9	64.6	13.5	18.5	20.3

Source: OECD (2011).

It follows that people retiring at the normal state retirement age will need to accumulate a larger stock of savings to carry through into retirement in order to finance their post-retirement spending. And the amounts are potentially large. For instance, some illustrative calculations by Coen Teulings and Richard Baldwin (2014) suggest that the stock of savings would need to rise by around one year's GDP to accommodate the increase in longevity over the past couple of decades. Of course, higher savings is not the only margin along which households could choose to adjust. People could choose to work beyond the normal state retirement age if they have not yet accumulated enough savings. And they may also decide to keep working for social reasons. So the effect on savings may be rather less than Teulings and Baldwin's calculations suggest. Even so, it is clear that population ageing could account for a significant increase in individual savings propensities.

Second, after a post-war bulge in births, couples have tended to have fewer children. Together with the increase in longevity, that has resulted in major changes in the age structure of populations. The implications of this evolving age structure for aggregate savings are potentially complex, but we can see the basic principles at work if we split an adult's life into three stages: young, characterised by relatively low wages; middle-aged, corresponding to the peak earning years; and old, corresponding to retirement. A lack of collateral means the young are likely to have only limited ability to borrow against their future income to finance consumption; we can think of this group as consuming what they earn. But as they move through into the high-earning middle period of their lives, they can start saving with a view to building up enough wealth to support themselves in retirement. Then, after retiring, they gradually run down their accumulated assets. Consequently, the difference in the population shares of the middle- and old-aged cohorts is central to determining aggregate savings propensities.[3]

Figure 2.4 shows the past and prospective evolution of the population shares of the middle-aged (40-64 years of age) and old (65 years and older) for the world excluding China, and for China (the size and rapid demographic evolution of China make it worth separating out). The figure also shows the difference between the two cohort shares, as this is what really matters. This difference has been rising for the past couple of decades, though it is presently around its peak and is projected to fall quite sharply over the next three decades. We consider the implications of this inflection point later, but for now we merely note the strong coincidence of the upward leg of the cohort share difference with the trend downwards in real interest rates. In other words, a demographic explanation passes the timing test.

As an additional piece of evidence on the potential importance of demographic pressures on savings propensities, Figure 2.5 shows a cross-country scatter plot of national savings rates against the respective national difference in cohort shares for successive five-year periods. There is a clear (and statistically significant) positive relationship between the two. That suggests demography is indeed a relevant factor in determining aggregate savings propensities.[4]

---

3   If the population shares of the young, middle-aged and old are $(1 - \alpha - \beta)$, α and β respectively, and the corresponding savings rates are 0, σ and $-\delta$ (with $\alpha, \beta, \sigma, \delta > 0$), then the aggregate savings rate will be $\alpha\sigma - \beta\delta = (\alpha - \beta)\sigma + \beta(\sigma - \delta)$.

4   Note that the finding that cross-country differences in savings rates can be partly accounted for by cross-country demographic differences is entirely consistent with the broad stability of global savings rates, as the consequent downward pressure on savings rates associated with the decline in the world real interest rate will have reduced savings in all jurisdictions together.

Figure 2.4   Past and projected population shares

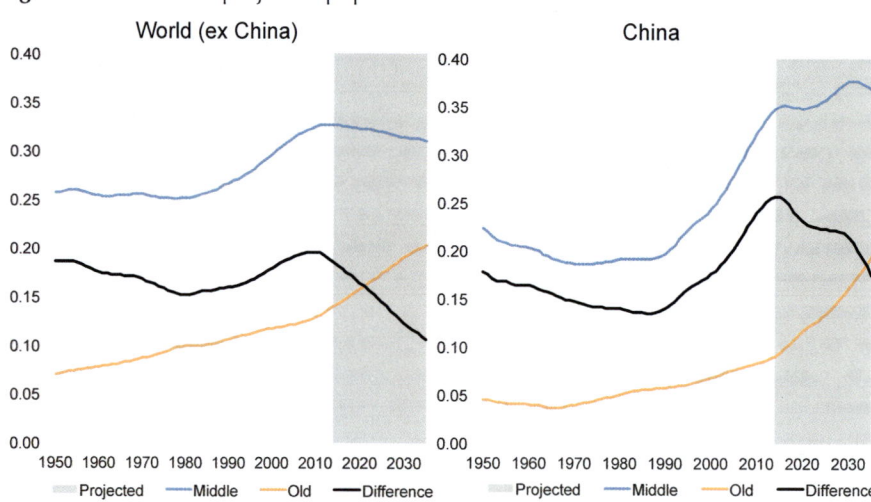

Source: United Nations.

Figure 2.5   Demographic pressure and savings propensities

Savings/GDP

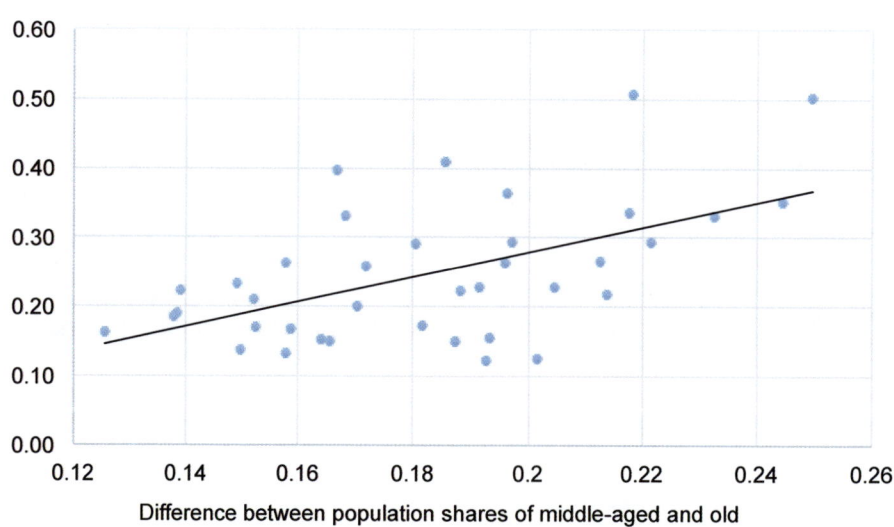

Difference between population shares of middle-aged and old

Notes: Observations are averages for the US, China, Eurozone (Germany, France, Italy, Spain, and Ireland), Japan, UK, India, Korea, Brazil, Mexico, and Russia over the following five-year periods: 1995-1999, 2000-2004, 2005-2009, and 2010-2014.

Source: United Nations and IMF WEO database.

Income distribution

Another possible driver of a higher propensity to save comes from shifts in the distribution of income. In many countries, the distribution of income has become more unequal over the past three decades or so. Figure 2.6 shows estimates of the Gini coefficient for the distribution of net income (i.e. after redistribution through the tax and benefit system) for a selection of advanced economies, taken from Frederick Solt's database (Solt, 2014). In all four countries, this measure has risen since the 1980s (the cross-country differences are in large part the consequence of differences in the extent of redistribution through the tax and benefit system). Similar trends can be observed in many other countries.

The cause of this rise in inequality is still a matter of debate. In part, it may reflect increased competition from labour-rich developing countries, such as China, which weakened the bargaining power of relatively unskilled labour in the advanced economies. But the lion's share is more likely to be down to technological developments, particularly in information and communications technology, that have allowed the jobs of unskilled and semi-skilled workers to be automated. Such technological advances have also allowed those with special abilities and skills ('superstars') to service a larger market, enabling them to capture a greater share of the returns accruing to such skills.

Figure 2.6   Inequality in selected economies

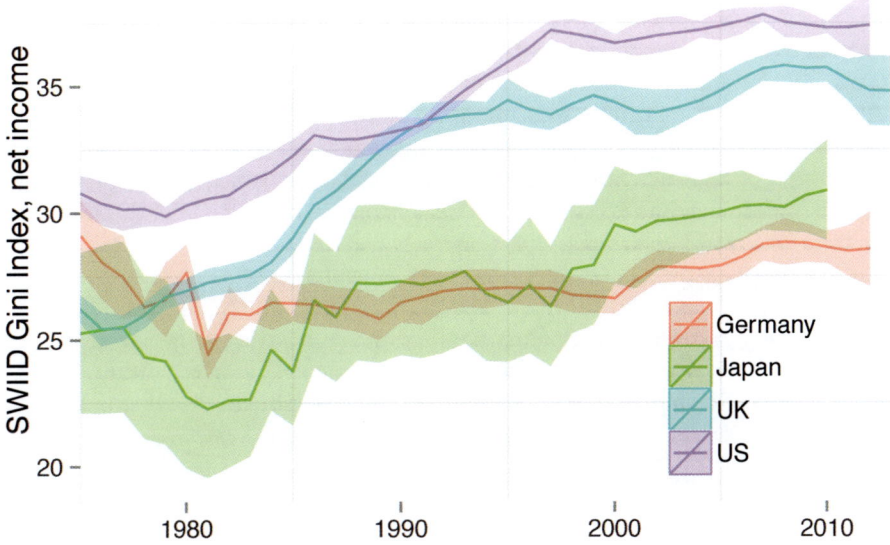

Note: Solid lines indicate mean estimates; shaded areas give 95% confidence bands.
Source: Solt (2014).

Whatever the cause of this increase in inequality, if high-income individuals have a higher propensity to save than low-income individuals, then the consequence of increased inequality will be a higher aggregate propensity to save. The rise in income inequality is, however, something that started almost two decades before long-term real interest rates began to drift down, suggesting that this may be less of a driver of the decline in long-term interest rates over the past couple of decades.

High savings in China

Figure 2.2 already hinted at the potential importance of the increase in the savings propensities of the emerging economies, especially China, in driving down global interest rates – the rise in the former aligning almost perfectly with the start of the downward trend in the latter. But why did savings rates rise so sharply in China? Commentators often cite the lack of household safety nets together with underdeveloped financial markets leading to high levels of self-insurance by households and a heavy reliance on internally generated funds on the part of businesses. These did not, however, become even less effective in the 1990s.

Instead, we believe it is more useful to look at the *interaction* of such factors with the demographic shifts we have already discussed. Indeed, as the right-hand panel of Figure 2.4 showed, the demographic shifts have been particularly large in China, in part perhaps because of the decline in fertility generated by the 'one child' policy; World Bank data suggest that the fertility rate in China fell from 2.63 births per woman in 1980 to just 1.61 in 2009. In addition, longevity has also risen sharply. In practice, support through extended family networks often represents the primary household insurance mechanism when state safety nets are underdeveloped, and China is probably no exception. With people living longer and smaller families, these networks become less able to provide an effective safety net for the elderly and unlucky. As a consequence, the incentive for households to build larger savings buffers increases.

It seems plausible that this interaction between demography and support networks therefore lies behind the sharp rise in Chinese saving over the past 15 years. In addition, households may also have been slow to increase their spending during a period of particularly rapid income growth, either because habits are slow to change or because they may hold off buying some goods in the expectation that if they wait then they will be able to buy better quality products in the future.

Chinese financial integration

This is, though, not the only way that developments in China may have affected global capital markets. The past couple of decades were marked not only by an increase in Chinese savings but also by a structural movement from financial autarky towards greater financial integration, paralleling – though lagging –

the process of trade integration. That process has been subject to considerable management by the state and still has some way to run.

The simple loanable funds framework shown in Figure 2.1 implicitly assumed that national capital markets were fully integrated. In such a world of perfect and frictionless capital mobility, the pool of global savings is just the sum of all the national savings pools, so that the corresponding global savings rate is just a weighted average of national savings rates, where the weights are each countries' shares in global output (this is what appears in Figure 2.2). Under integration, the global savings rate therefore rises either when a country's savings rate rises or when a country with an above-average savings rate grows faster than average so that its output share rises.

In contrast, under financial autarky it makes no sense to talk about a pool of global savings. There are instead just a series of national (or regional) pools of savings and investment with corresponding national (or regional) real interest rates. When those capital markets integrate, we should expect real interest rates in the different jurisdictions to be driven together, with capital flowing from the nations or regions where interest rates were initially low to jurisdictions where the returns are higher. This is just the analogue of what happens to the prices of tradable goods and services as countries open up their markets to international trade.

The process is illustrated in Figure 2.7, which generalises the simple loanable funds apparatus of Figure 2.1 to two separate regions: call them the 'advanced economies' and the 'emerging economies'. We begin in financial autarky, with corresponding equilibrium real interest rates of r_A and r_E respectively. As drawn, the equilibrium real interest rate under autarky is lower in the emerging economies than in the advanced economies. With financial integration, there is a single world interest rate, r^*, such that capital outflows from the emerging economies, x, exactly match the inflow into the advanced economies, also x. Clearly, if interest rates under autarky are such that r_A is lower than r_E, then capital would flow in the other direction. When financial integration is only partial, then the outcome will lie somewhere between the two extremes: the regional interest rates will be pushed towards each other but need not necessarily converge.

Figure 2.7 Effect of financial integration

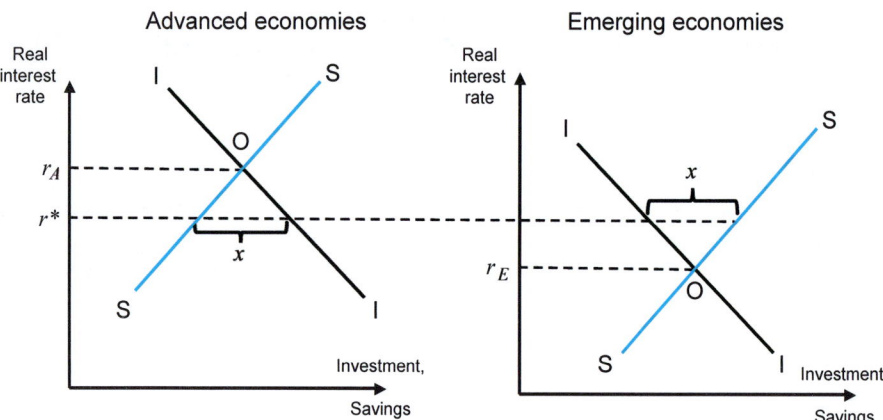

What we called the 'world real interest rate' in Chapter 1 should more accurately have been labelled the 'advanced economy real interest rate'. Unfortunately, the various controls on the financial sector and data limitations mean that it is difficult, if not impossible, to obtain an estimate of the Chinese real interest rate under autarky that would be comparable. We are therefore forced to rely on indirect inference.

We start by documenting the growing importance of China in the world economy and in international capital markets. The first two columns of Table 2.2 show the shares of the top ten countries in world GDP in 1990, when Chinese integration into the world economy was still quite limited, and then for last year; China rises from tenth to second. The final two columns show the corresponding shares of foreign direct investment; China was not even in the top ten in 1990, but had risen to fifth by 2014 (and second if Hong Kong is also included).

FDI is, of course, only one component of international capital movements – portfolio movements and reserve accumulation do not figure, for instance. And reserve accumulation has been a major feature of this period, not only by China but also, though to a lesser extent, by some other emerging economies. In part, that has been fuelled by an understandable desire to increase the ability to self-insure after being compelled to turn to the IMF for support during the 1997-1998 Asian financial crisis. But the scale of the Chinese accumulation of reserves, which currently stand at around $4 trillion (equivalent to twice annual imports) with much of it in US Treasuries, goes beyond what can be regarded as necessary just for self-insurance. Instead, some of the past accumulation is likely to be the by-product of a development strategy that was heavily export-driven.

Table 2.2 GDP and FDI shares

	Share of GDP			Share of FDI		
	1990		2014		1990		2014

	1990		2014		1990		2014
US	29.9	US	25.3	Japan	20.2	US	27.2
Japan	15.5	China	15.0	UK	18.9	Japan	8.2
Germany	7.7	Japan	6.9	US	18.2	Hong Kong	7.0
France	6.4	Germany	5.5	France	9.5	Germany	6.8
Italy	5.7	France	4.2	N'lands	6.0	China	6.4
UK	5.1	UK	4.1	Sweden	5.0	Russia	5.0
Canada	3.0	Brazil	3.3	Canada	3.7	France	4.5
Spain	2.6	Italy	3.1	Australia	2.9	UK	3.7
Brazil	2.3	Russia	3.0	Belgium	2.5	Canada	3.7
China	2.0	India	3.0	Italy	2.4	N'lands	2.9
Top 10	*80.3*	*Top 10*	*73.4*	*Top 10*	*89.3*	*Top 10*	*75.4*

Source: IMF.

As a simple heuristic that captures this broader concept of financial integration, we first note that a key driver for the rise in international financial cross-holdings has been the substantial increase in international trade. Now the usual global savings measure – of the sort shown in Figure 2.2 – weights together national savings rates by GDP shares; such a measure assumes national markets are completely integrated and there is a single pool of savings. If a country is not integrated at all, it should clearly get a zero weight in a measure of global savings. And if a country is becoming more integrated, that should be reflected in a weight that rises faster that its GDP share. So, to construct an indicator of 'financially integrated' global savings, we construct a weighted savings measure, where the weights are obtained by *interacting* trade $(T_i/\overline{T})$ and GDP $(Y_i/\overline{Y})$ shares with $\overline{T} = \Sigma_i\, T_i$ and $\overline{Y} = \Sigma_i\, Y_i$:

$$w_i \equiv \frac{(Y_i/\overline{Y})\,(T_i/\overline{T})}{\Sigma_i\,(Y_i/\overline{Y})\,(T_i/\overline{T})}$$

Figure 2.8 shows this indicator of 'financially integrated' savings, together with the conventionally measured global savings rate. The former rises much faster over the past decade or so. The rising shares of trade of China and India (countries with high savings rates) and the falling shares of advanced economies (with low savings rates) mean that the financially integrated pool of savings grows more rapidly than the usual measure. This reinforces the idea that the pool of global savings has risen sharply over the past couple of decades.

Figure 2.8   'Financially integrated' savings rate

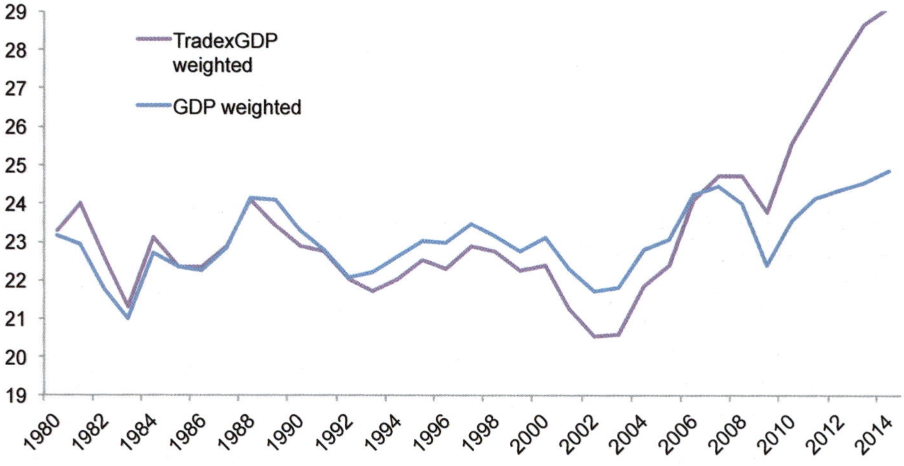

Source: IMF and own calculations.

By itself, this does not tell us anything about the impact of Chinese financial integration on global real interest rates; it depends on whether integration on the savings side has been rising faster or slower than integration on the investment side. In the former case, it exerts downward pressure; in the latter case, it produces upward pressure. The key fact, however, is that capital has been flowing out of China – the counterpart of the Chinese current account deficit – so that China is, on net, adding to the pool of savings available for investment elsewhere. As Figure 2.7 suggests, that is consistent with the Chinese interest rate under autarky being below the rate obtaining in the rest of the world, and financial integration in practice having added to the downward pressure on world real interest rates.

After-effects of the financial crisis

As noted in Chapter 1, the decline in long-term real interest rates is not primarily a consequence of the financial crisis but a more long-standing phenomenon. There are several factors, however, that have come into play since the crisis. Private savings in the advanced economies rose substantially, for several reasons. First, the adverse shock to income expectations and increased uncertainty led to higher household saving. And that rise in savings appears to have been particularly pronounced among highly indebted households. Figure 2.9, for instance, shows that in the UK, the rise in household savings was concentrated amongst those households with particularly large mortgages relative to their income.

Figure 2.9 UK savings rates by household type[a]

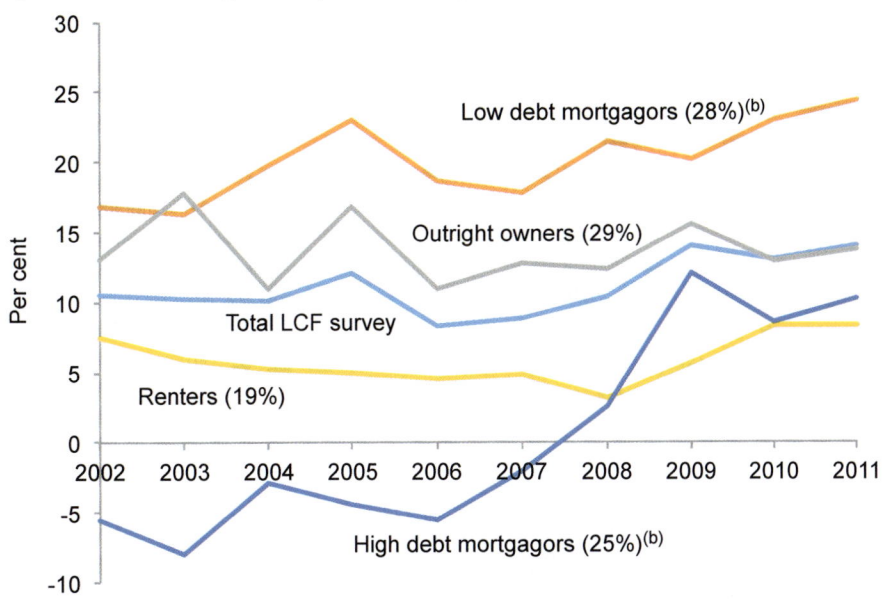

Notes: (a) Saving ratios calculated using the average consumption and disposable income levels for each group of households. Numbers in parentheses show their share of total income in 2007. (b) High-debt mortgagors are defined as having outstanding mortgage debt of more than twice their annual disposable income. All other mortgagors are low debt.

Source: May 2013 *Inflation Report*, Bank of England.

Turning to businesses, in the US and several other advanced economies, the net financial asset position of the corporate sector had been rising since well before the financial crisis (Armenter, 2012; Karabarbounis and Neiman, 2012). The reasons for this are not yet fully understood, though they may relate to the increased value of having a pool of liquid assets available to buffer shocks to a firm's cash flow, rather than adjusting along other margins, such as reducing dividends. In any case, the crisis seems to have accentuated that trend, with firms continuing to accumulate liquid financial assets, rather than investing them in physical capital or distributing them to shareholders. The driver here seems to have been companies' (especially smaller businesses') bad experience during the credit crunch that accompanied the financial crisis – owners and managers learnt that bank credit lines and market sources of finance could evaporate just when they were most needed. That made self-insurance, rather than reliance on external finance, appear even more sensible.

Finally, although household savings rates have eased back down in some countries as output has firmed, there has also been a countervailing shift towards fiscal consolidation that has helped to keep national savings rates elevated.

2.2   A lower propensity to invest

Turning now to the investment side of the equation, there are also several reasons why the propensity to invest may have declined.

Demography

Just as demographic developments may have boosted savings rates in recent years, they may also have had an impact on the rate of investment. In particular, at the same time as people are living longer, they are generally having fewer children. The consequence has been a steady fall in the rate of the growth of the working-age population since the mid-1980s (see Figure 2.10). Labour force growth has consequently fallen back, though in some countries that has been mitigated by an increase in labour force participation, particularly that of females.

Figure 2.10 Working age (20-64 years) population growth (five-year averages)

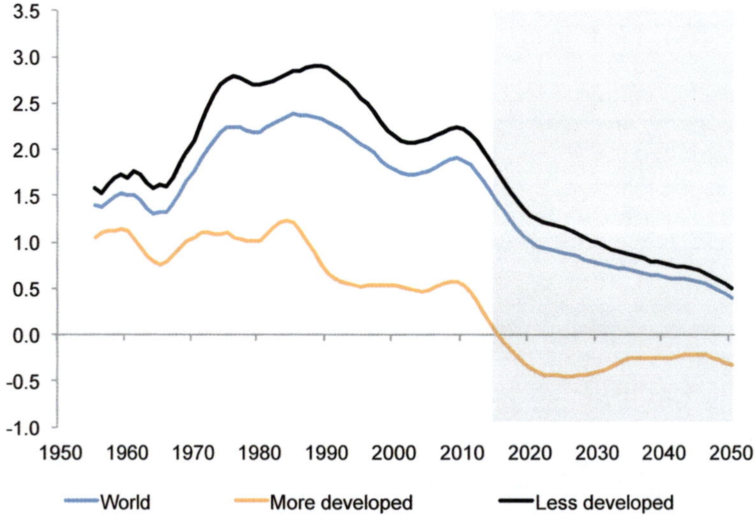

Source: UN database.

The impact of this on investment is potentially complex. For a given capital-labour ratio, a lower rate of growth of the workforce automatically translates into a lower required rate of growth of the capital stock, which would reduce investment demand. But, against that, a relative scarcity of labour will tend to push up pay and encourage businesses to substitute capital for labour, thus raising investment. The net impact on the demand for capital is thus unclear.

In any case, the fall in population growth rates seems to predate the fall in real interest rates by a decade or more. So this particular mechanism appears to fail the timing test. It therefore seems unlikely to be a major contributor to the decline in the world real interest rate.

A decline in the rate of innovation

As mentioned in Box 2.1, Robert Gordon has argued that the rate of growth of potential output is likely to slow in the US and other advanced economies, in part because of the demographic effects just discussed but also because the rate of innovation is likely to be permanently lower. He points out the rapid growth of the past 250 years since the start of the Industrial Revolution has been on the back of three fundamental sets of innovations: the steam engine and the railroads; electricity and the internal combustion engine; and the digital revolution. But he is pessimistic that the future will bring more such fundamental advances. As a result, he argues, the rate of total factor productivity growth is slowing back towards the much slower rates that obtained before the Industrial Revolution. And in turn that has diminished the propensity to invest, and will continue to do so. Other authors have expounded related ideas, most notably Tyler Cowen (2011).

It is indeed the case that productivity growth (both output per person-hour and total factor productivity) has been weak over the past few years in countries such as the UK and the US. But much of this appears to be a legacy of the financial crisis and thus seems likely to prove temporary rather than secular.[5] Moreover, authors such as Erik Brynjolfsson and Andrew McAfee (2011) have pointed to the major changes being wrought by the digital revolution, whose effects are only just beginning to be felt. And, as documented by Joel Moykr (2013), several other recent scientific advances offer tantalising future possibilities too. Finally it is worth recalling just how poor human beings have been in the past at seeing the scope for future advancement. Even experts can be way off the mark in their crystal-ball gazing – as the quotations in Box 2.2 attest!

Box 2.2   It is not so easy to foresee the future…

"Heavier-than-air flying machines are impossible."
(Lord Kelvin, President of the Royal Society, 1895)

"Everything that can be invented has been invented."
(Charles Duell, Commissioner, US Office of Patents, 1899)

"The wireless music box has no imaginable commercial value. Who would pay for a message sent to nobody in particular?"
(David Sarnoff Associates, 1920s)

"Who the hell wants to hear actors talk?"
(Head of Warner Brothers, 1927)

"I think there is a world market for maybe five computers."
(Thomas Watson, Chairman of IBM, 1943)

"There is no reason anyone would want a computer in their home."
(Ken Olsen, Chairman of DEC, 1977)

---

5   Note that this does not imply the shortfall in the level of productivity relative to a continuation of the pre-crisis trend will be made up.

Consequently, we are inclined to place little weight on the argument that the rate of innovation has slowed permanently, especially when the digital revolution probably has some way to run and new technologies like genetic engineering are still very much in their infancy. That, however, does not rule out innovation and total factor productivity growth remaining temporarily depressed as an after-effect of the financial crisis.

Changes in the nature of growth

In some industries, the nature of the production process is such that it relies much more on highly skilled individuals (i.e. human capital) rather than physical capital that substitutes for repetitive activities by workers. Obvious examples are finance and software development. The increased importance of software companies such as Google in the business activity of advanced economies, as well as to the development and use of products such as smart phones, will therefore tend to lower the incremental (physical) capital-output ratio. Moreover, a shortage of individuals with the technical skills necessary to use such innovative technologies may also discourage whatever investment in physical capital is needed to exploit new technologies (see Jorgenson et al., 2014). Whether this is a large enough phenomenon at the macroeconomic level to explain the fall in long-term real interest rates is, however, more debatable.

Falling relative price of capital goods

Another explanation for a decline in the demand for funds for capital investment stems from the falling relative price of capital goods. This is a long-established trend that is present in most countries and, in the first instance, derives from the fact that productivity growth is generally faster in manufacturing than in services, though more recently it may also be associated with the exploitation of advances in information technology. As a consequence, the user cost of capital has been trending downwards (see Karababounis and Nieman, 2012). This will encourage higher real investment, but also a decline in the *nominal* demand for funds to invest provided that the elasticity of the demand for capital with respect to the cost of capital is sufficiently low.

This particular hypothesis suffers from two weaknesses, however. First, it is not clear why the long-term real interest rate should have only started trending down in the late 1990s when the relative price of investment goods appears to have been falling since the early 1970s (see, for example, Thwaites, 2014). So the argument fails the timing test. Moreover, because the lower user cost of capital encourages more *real* investment, it should also have raised the growth of real output, which did not obviously happen.

After-effects of the financial crisis

Just as there have been factors raising savings in advanced economies during the period since the financial crisis, so investment – which fell sharply after

2008, reflecting the deterioration in prospects and heightened uncertainty – has remained subdued. Such behaviour is typical after large crises, as documented by Carmen Reinhart and Ken Rogoff (2009). Confidence can take a long time to recover and the irreversibility of investment is likely to make businesses reluctant to undertake investment, particularly to expand capacity, until they can be confident that there will be enough demand for their products. And while the 15 to 20 years before the crisis – the Great Moderation – was a generally benign environment from a macroeconomic perspective, the experience since then, with the Eurozone debt crisis following hard on the heels of the 2007-2008 banking crisis, has surely encouraged businesses to be remain cautious, lest the future bring yet another crisis in some other part of the globe. Uncertainty about fiscal and regulatory policy following the crisis also may have contributed to firms' reluctance to invest (e.g. Baker et al., 2013).

It seems entirely plausible that this weakness in investment is a significant factor behind a further decline in the natural real interest rate since the start of the crisis (remember that the natural rate will have been even lower than the observed rate in the markets once the zero lower bound on policy rates was reached). Moreover, as noted earlier, there was a marked fall in the global savings/ investment rate during the Great Recession (see Figure 2.2). So we think it natural to ascribe at least some of the decline in yields since 2008 to this.

2.3   Risky versus safe assets and portfolio shifts

There is, then, no shortage of hypotheses couched in terms of shifts in the propensities to save or invest capable of explaining the downward pressure on long-term risk-free real interest rates. There is, however, another class of hypotheses warranting consideration. These rest on shifts in preferences for, or supplies of, different types of asset. In particular, a shift in preferences towards safe assets or a reduction in their supply can be expected to lead to upward pressure on the price of safe assets and a fall in their yields, with the converse effect on the prices of risky assets and on the corresponding risk premia.

Demand for safe assets

We already noted above that the desire to hold larger foreign-exchange buffers following the Asian financial crisis was one factor behind the increase in emerging economy saving, as well being a by-product of the Chinese trade surplus. But this increase in holdings of foreign-exchange reserves was heavily concentrated in holdings of US Treasuries.

There has surely been a further increase in the demand for safe assets as a consequence of the financial crisis; that investors are likely to turn to safe assets in times of heightened uncertainty is standard fare in macroeconomics. But while it is difficult to get much action in standard models from a *general* increase in uncertainty – that is, a two-sided increase in the spread of possible outcomes – it is possible to get quantitatively more significant effects if there is just an increase in the likelihood or size of *bad* outcomes. Robert Barro (2006, 2009), in particular, has shown how disaster risk – low-probability catastrophic events – can generate both low risk-free rates and a high equity premium. And surely the move from Great Moderation to Great Panic and then Great Recession must have made investors more aware of the possibility of such events. Ben Broadbent (2014) and David Miles (2014) have argued that this provides yet another factor behind the current low level of risk-free real interest rates.

In addition, during the years preceding the crisis, banks had run down their holdings of liquid assets to extraordinarily low levels. Figure 2.11 provides some relevant data for the UK banking sector. Regulators have responded to the weaknesses exposed by the crisis by requiring banks not only to carry more loss-absorbing capacity but also to ensure that they have an adequate stock of unencumbered high-quality liquid assets that can be converted easily and immediately in private markets into cash in the event of a month-long stress event (the liquidity coverage ratio). To all intents and purposes, 'safe' and 'liquid' are synonymous (though what is safe and liquid may vary over time). These new regulatory standards have further added to the demand for safe assets and, as the transition to the new requirement is still in train, will continue to do so for the next few years. Tightened prudential requirements on pension funds and insurance companies in some jurisdictions, forcing them to match their assets better to their liabilities, will also have further added to the demand for safe bonds.

Figure 2.11   Sterling liquid assets of UK banking sector[a]

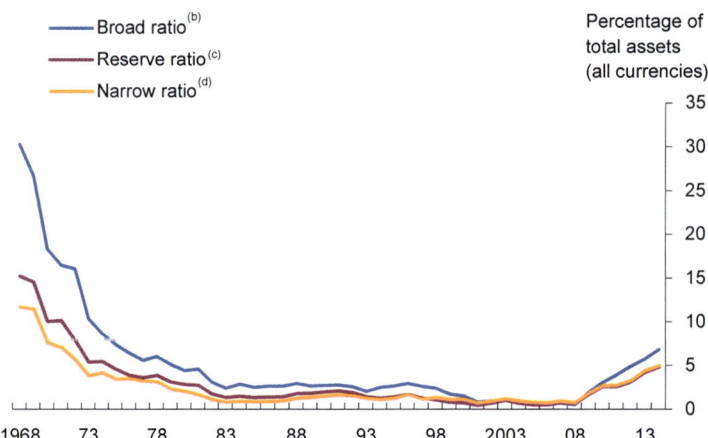

Notes: (a) Data for building societies are included. Prior to this, data are for UK banks only. Data are year-end except for 2013 where end-November data are used. (b) Broad ratio: Cash + Bank of England balances + money at call + eligible bills + UK gilts. (c) Reserve ratio proxied by Bank of England balances + money at call + eligible bills. (d) Narrow ratio: Cash + Bank of England balances + eligible bills.

Source: Bank of England.

Finally, central bank asset purchases ('quantitative easing') have provided a further source of demand. The purpose of those asset-purchase programmes was precisely to depress the term premium on longer-term risk-free assets when short-term rates had attained the zero lower bound. The consequent portfolio rebalancing as investors substituted towards higher-yielding assets was then expected to raise asset prices generally and lower the corresponding yields, so boosting demand. Event studies suggest that the effect of the first rounds of asset purchases by the Federal Reserve and the Bank of England during the Great Recession was to lower long-term risk-free yields by roughly 100 basis points (see Chapter 4 for further discussion), though the impact of later rounds of purchases is somewhat harder to pin down.

Supply of safe assets

The strong demand for safe assets before (and even more so after) the crisis meant there were incentives for the financial industry to find ways of increasing the supply of such assets by repackaging and income flows and redistributing risks to those better able to bear them. Ahead of the crisis, this was manifested in the repackaging of the returns on mortgage-backed securities and similar assets so that the safer tranches could then be held by investors with a low appetite for risk, such as pension funds. But the events of 2007-2008 revealed that such assets – despite their AAA ratings – were anything but safe in the face of falling house prices and correlated defaults. Moreover, the subsequent Eurozone debt crisis and the determination of some member countries to ensure that sovereign debt obligations are not mutualised has also led to the re-emergence of significant risk premia on the sovereign debt of periphery countries and other member states with elevated debt or deficits. Consequently, some assets that were perceived as safe before the crisis no longer warrant that label, making them ineligible for some classes of investor.

Table 2.3, taken from Caballero and Farhi (2014), suggests that the fall in the supply of safe assets is significant: from 37% of world GDP in 2007 to 18% in 2011, according to their particular definition of 'safe'. It is worth pointing out, however, that this is a rather narrow definition, excluding as it does the sovereign debt of countries such as the UK and Japan. It also excludes measures of short-term deposits or cash, which are particularly safe assets. Moreover, the sharp rise in fiscal deficits since the crisis means that the supply of sovereign assets has been rising rapidly in the past few years.

Table 2.3 Decline in supply of 'safe' assets

	US$ trn		% of world GDP	
	2007	2011	2007	2011
US sovereign debt	5.1	10.7	9.2	15.8
o/w held by Federal Reserve	0.7	1.7	1.3	2.5
German & French sovereign debt	2.4	3.3	4.5	4.8
Italian & Spanish sovereign debt	2.4	3.1	4.3	4.7
US MBS and ABS	11.3	9.6	20.2	14.2
'Safe' assets	20.5	12.3	36.9	18.1

Source: Caballero and Farhi (2014).

Incorporating risky assets into the loanable funds apparatus

To integrate this dimension into our analysis, we need to extend our elementary loanable funds apparatus to accommodate multiple assets and interest rates. Making the heroic simplifying assumption that sovereign bonds – and *only* sovereign bonds – are safe, we can write two loanable funds equilibrium conditions:

Risky assets:
$$f(\rho)S_{private}(r, r + \rho, ...) = I(r + \rho, ...)$$
$$\underset{(+)}{}\quad \underset{(+)\;(+)}{}\quad\quad\quad \underset{(-)}{}$$

Safe assets:
$$[1 - f(\rho)]S_{private}(r, r + \rho, ...) + S_{public} = 0$$

where r is the yield on safe assets; ρ is the spread of the expected return on risky capital assets over the return on the safe asset; and the share of funds allocated to risky assets, $f(\rho)$, is increasing in that spread ($f' > 0$). For simplicity, we take the public primary deficit, $-S_{public}$, as independent of the level of interest rates. Adding these two equations together gives the conventional loanable funds relationship:

Loanable funds:
$$S_{private}(r, r + \rho, ...) + S_{public} = I(r + \rho, ...) \qquad \text{(IS)}$$

while taking their ratio gives a funds allocation relationship that is key to determining the spread:

Funds allocation:
$$\varphi(\rho) \equiv f(\rho)/[1 - f(\rho)] = -I(r + \rho, ...)/S_{public} \qquad \text{(FF)}$$

Figure 2.12 shows the equilibrium of this little system in $\{r, \rho\}$ space. IS plots the risk-free interest rate and spread pairs that are consistent with equilibrium in the overall market for loanable funds. It slopes downward, but the slope is greater than unity in absolute magnitude. Exogenous increases in saving or decreases in investment shift the IS schedule to the left.

Figure 2.12 Equilibrium with safe and risky assets

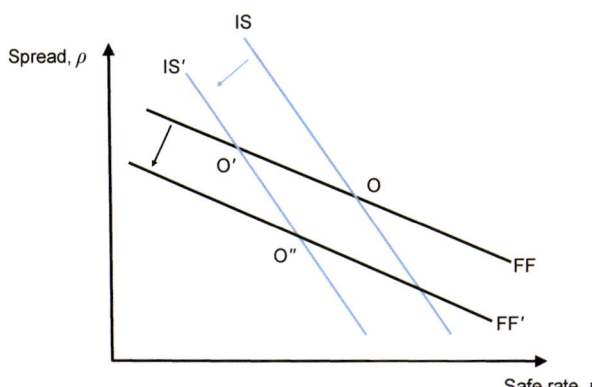

FF plots the risk-free interest rate and spread pairs consistent with the allocation of funds. It too slopes downward, but the absolute value of the slope is less than unity. It is unaffected by exogenous changes in private saving, but exogenous reductions in investment also shift it to the left. And a shift in the allocation of funds towards safe assets would shift FF up.

An exogenous increase in private savings thus takes the economy from O to O'; it is therefore consistent with a fall in the risk-free rate and an increase in the spread. By contrast, an exogenous reduction in investment takes the economy from O to O'' and a little bit of algebra establishes that the spread in this case necessarily falls – as one would intuitively expect. Finally, a shift in the allocation of funds in favour of safe assets would in effect move the economy from O'' to O', depressing the safe rate and raising the spread.

Evidence

A rise in investor preference for safe assets should be reflected in investors demanding a higher spread between risky and safe assets. But the empirical analogue of the spread between risky and safe assets can take several forms. We start by looking at a measure of the equity risk premium, that is, the return on risky equities relative to that on safe sovereign bonds. We focus on the US and the UK as we have a decent run of returns on indexed sovereign debt in each case (see Figure 2.13). As the measure of the stock returns, we take the (inverted) stock price-to-earnings ratio, scaled by the ratio of the value of firm equity to the sum of that valuation and net debt. It therefore measures corporate earnings relative to the *total* finance provided (equity plus debt), and so gives an estimate of the yield on capital unaffected by variations in leverage.

Figure 2.13 Safe sovereign and equity yields

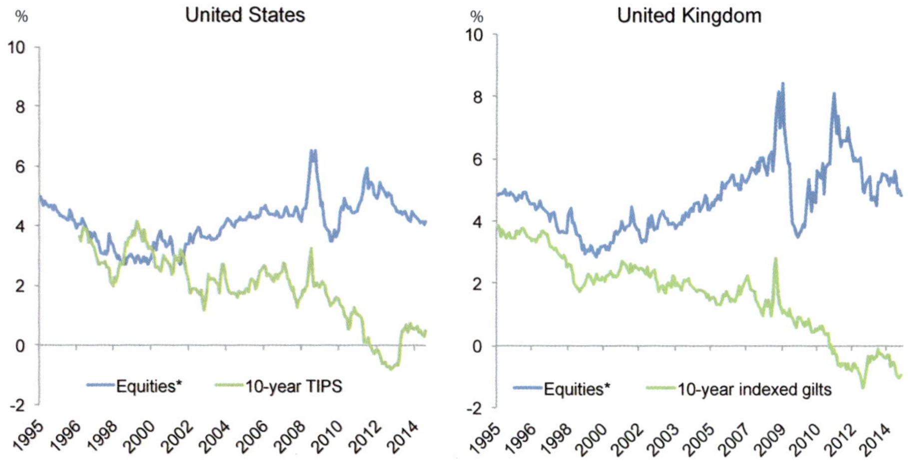

Note: *Leverage-adjusted inverted price-earnings ratio.
Source: Bank of England, following Broadbent (2014).

The results are quite striking. While the real return on indexed sovereign debt trends steadily downwards, our measure of the return on capital has been broadly flat to rising in both countries since the late 1990s, consistent with a rising preference for safe assets. Different factors are likely to have been work at different times, however. Risk premia rise noticeably after the collapse of the US tech bubble in 2000 and especially after the 2007-2008 financial crisis, both periods of heightened stress when we might expect a shift in preferences towards safe assets. In the intervening period, the key factor is instead more likely to be the large Chinese trade surplus and the associated accumulation of reserve holdings, largely in the form of US Treasuries. But since the financial crisis, Chinese reserve accumulation has fallen back, so this is unlikely to have been much of a driving factor in the past few years.

We might also expect similar trends to be seen within fixed income assets, with the spread of the return on risky bonds rising relative to that on safe bonds. Figure 1.5 provided an estimate of the real return on the sovereign debt of a sample of emerging economies, and suggested that the spread relative to the advanced economy safe real rate had fallen sharply after the Asian financial crisis and thereafter had flattened off, or even risen a touch. Figure 2.14 provides more reliable information on this spread, namely, the J.P. Morgan EMBI+ credit option-adjusted spread relative to US Treasuries. This confirms the significant narrowing in the decade or so after the Asian financial crisis. Unsurprisingly, the spread spikes up in 2008 during the financial crisis. But a comparison of the spread immediately before and then after the crisis is instructive. Unlike equity risk premia, which rise markedly, the spread on emerging economy sovereign debt rises only a touch.

Figure 2.14 Emerging economies' sovereign credit spread

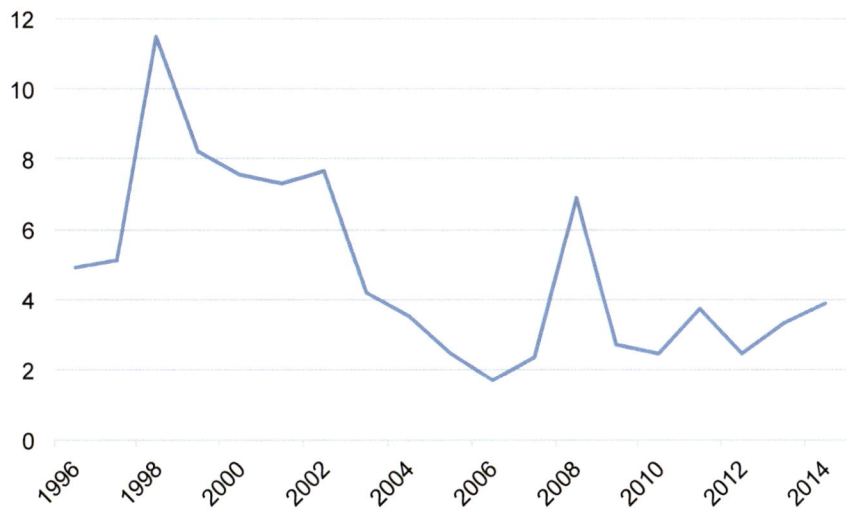

Source: J.P. Morgan EMBI+ credit option-adjusted spread.

This suggests more might have happened than just a shift in preferences towards safe assets. It is possible that the sovereign debts of at least some emerging economies are no longer seen as being quite as risky as they once were. In particular, the improvement in fiscal positions, as well as greater holdings of foreign exchange reserves, renders them less vulnerable to adverse shocks. That would also help to counteract – at least to some degree – the reduction in the supply of safe assets as a consequence of the rise in the perceived riskiness of advanced economy asset-backed securities and peripheral sovereign debt that Caballero and Farhi (2014) focus on. How durable this is remains to be seen, however. Certainly, the substantial outflows from emerging economies over the past year in the face of concerns about slowing growth in China and heightened expectations that policy rates will soon begin to rise in the US suggest they remain a somewhat risky asset class.

Turning to corporate fixed income returns, Figure 2.15 shows the spread of the return on risky high-yield corporate bonds over that on much safer investment-grade bonds. This shows a similar pattern to that for sovereign debt – leaving aside the 2008-2009 spike, there appears to be only a relatively modest increase in the spread compared to where it was before the crisis. Consequently, any increased preference for safety is much less obvious here than for equities. Overall it seems that the switch in preferences is more noticeable *across* asset classes than *within* asset classes.

Figure 2.15 US high-yield over investment-grade credit spread

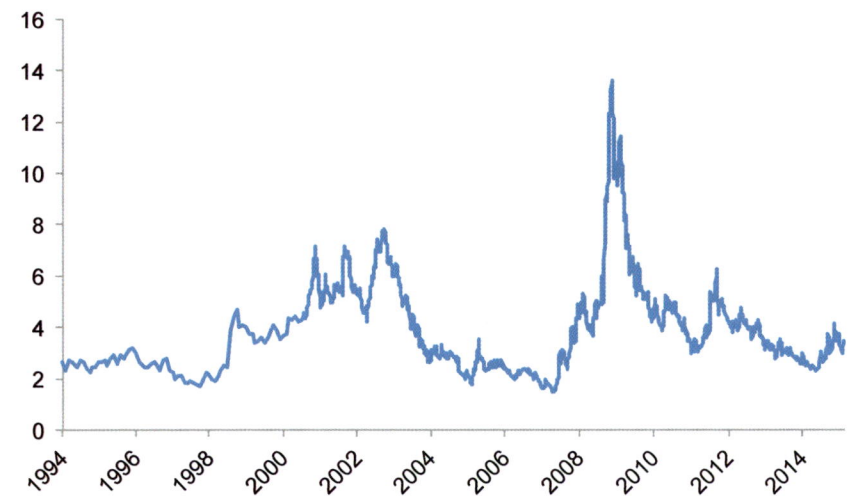

Source: : Bloomberg. US High yield proxy using Barclays US High Yield index option-adjusted spread; US Investment-grade credit proxy using Barclays US Investment-grade option-adjusted spread.

2.4 Summing up

Bringing together these various strands, we are led to conclude that there is no single driver of the decline in long-term risk-free real interest rates over the past two decades. Instead, different factors seem to have been more important at different times. In particular:

- Demographic pressure associated with increased longevity and lower fertility is likely to have been important, especially during the first half of the period. The surge in Chinese savings is likely to be a particular reflection of these demographic forces. But these pressures are likely to wane in coming years, as the population share of the high-saving middle-aged relative to that of dissaving retirees is presently around its peak.
- The gradual integration of China into global financial markets may have also placed downward pressure on the global real interest rate. The pattern of capital flowing 'uphill' from emerging to advanced economies is consistent with this explanation.
- While a decline in the propensity to invest seems less convincing as an explanation of the pre-crisis downward trend in real interest rates, it does seem likely to have played a role in explaining developments since 2008.
- Shifts in the supply of, and demand for, safe assets may also have placed downward pressure on the risk-free real rate, particularly since the financial crisis. This is consistent with the rise in equity risk premia in recent years, though some of the other evidence is less supportive.

In light of these conclusions, will the downward pressure on the equilibrium real interest rate be maintained, or should we expect the real rate to revert to the historical norm of roughly two per cent? We return to this question in Chapter 4, together with a consideration of some of the possible consequences should the present low interest rate environment persist. But before that, we undertake a case study of Japan, where the ageing of the population is more advanced than in most developed economies; experience there may therefore help us to see more clearly the implications of the demographic factors analysed above. In addition, Japan has already lived with low interest rates for more than a couple of decades. What lessons are contained in its experience?

3 Lessons from Japan

The experience of Japan since the bursting of the bubble in equity and property prices at the end of the 1980s provides a potentially illuminating case study. By the time the 2007-2008 financial crisis hit the rest of the advanced economies, Japanese policymakers had been grappling with the challenge of handling an environment of persistently low nominal and real interest rates for more than a decade. As discussed further in Chapter 4, a world of persistently low rates makes it more likely that monetary policy will be constrained by the (near) zero lower bound on policy rates, forcing central banks instead to turn to unconventional monetary policies, such as quantitative easing. Such an environment also puts more of the burden of sustaining aggregate demand on fiscal policy. Policymakers' attempts to escape the deflationary trap that Japan fell into after 1998 potentially provide an insight into the effectiveness of policy in such circumstances.

3.1 A brief chronology

Following the bursting of the twin equity and real estate price bubbles and the unwinding of the accompanying credit boom, Japan gradually fell into a prolonged period of disinflation, leading eventually to outright deflation. Equity prices peaked on the final business day of 1989 and real estate prices began to fall shortly thereafter. Over the next two years, output growth remained firm but then began to slow as the impact of lower asset prices and tighter monetary and fiscal policies (discussed below) were felt. By 1992, the economy had begun to stagnate, a condition that was to persist for the next 20 years – the 'two lost decades' – as real GDP grew at an average rate of just 1%, while nominal GDP remained broadly flat (see Figure 3.1). In addition, though it was not immediately recognised, the rate of growth of potential output also appears to have shifted down, from the heady rates of around 4% experienced in the 1970s and 1980s to something nearer 1% in the 1990s and 2000s.

After a short period of monetary tightening in 1990, both nominal and real interest rates fell steadily as the Bank of Japan sought to sustain demand (see Figures 3.2 and 3.3). By 1999, the Bank of Japan's policy rate had reached its effective floor. Except for a short period during 2006-2007, the policy rate has remained there ever since. Importantly, however, the behaviour of the real interest rate – which previously had moved in line with the nominal interest rate – now began to mirror the behaviour of inflation, rising when the latter fell and vice versa.

Figure 3.1   Japanese nominal and real GDP

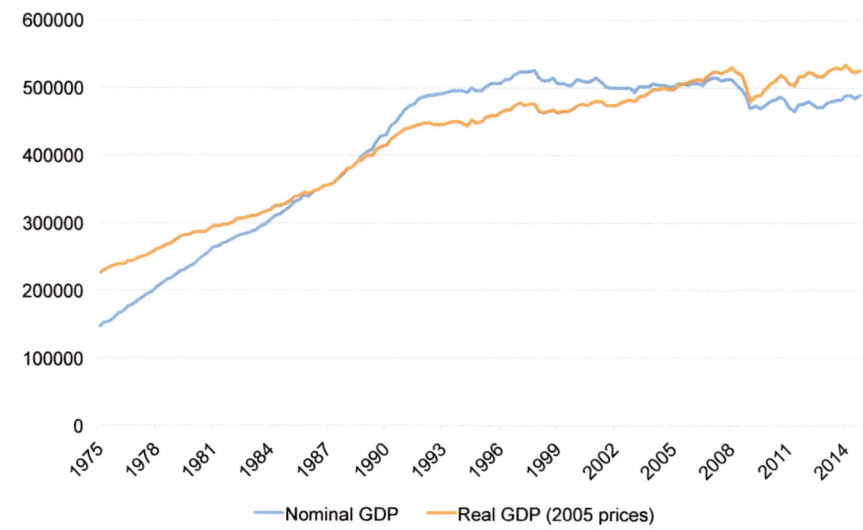

Source: Cabinet Office.

Figure 3.2   Japanese nominal interest rates

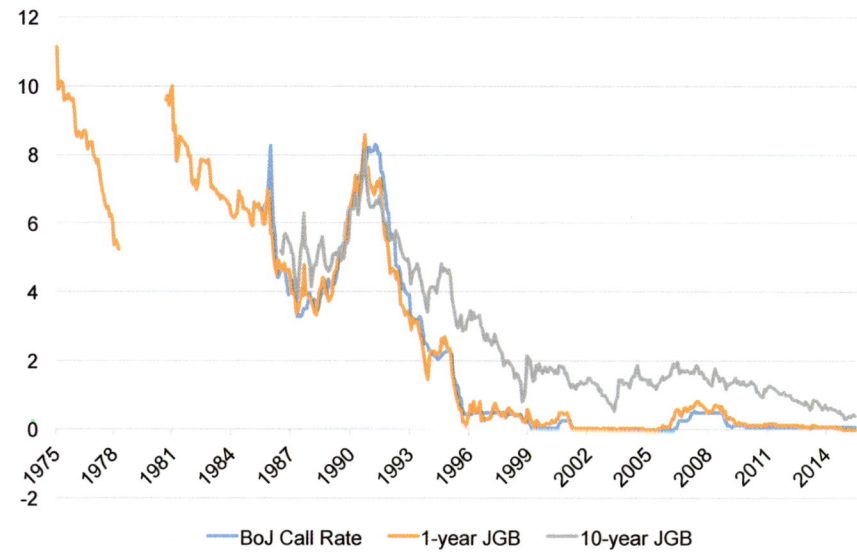

Source: Bank of Japan and Ministry of Finance.

Figure 3.3   Japanese real interest rates

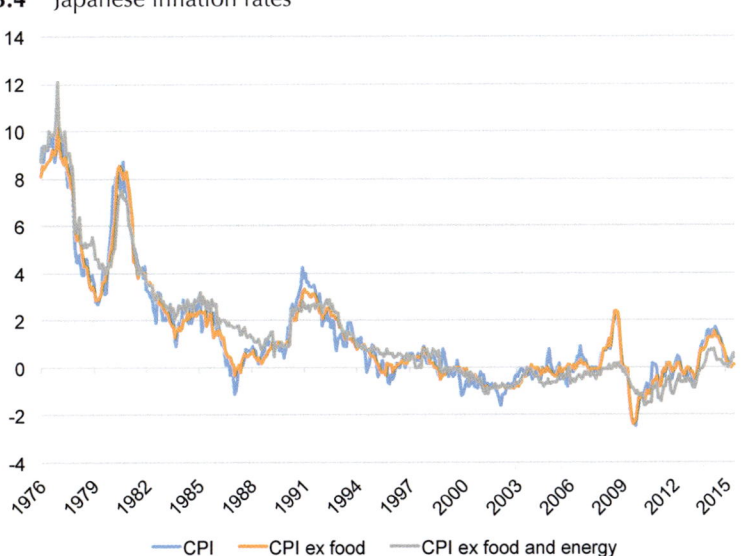

Source: Bank of Japan, Ministry of Finance and Statistics Japan.

Headline inflation reached 4.0% (and core inflation 3.2%) in January 1991 (Figure 3.4). That was significantly above the 1% or so of two years earlier. But the tightening in monetary policy and the slowdown in growth led inflation gradually to fall back, dipping to below 1% in April 1994. But instead of stabilising in the 1-2% range, inflation continued to drift down. By 1998, headline and core inflation had reached zero, ushering in a period of deflation that would last until 2012, save for a few months in 2007-2008.

Figure 3.4   Japanese inflation rates

Source: Statistics Japan.

Our discussion of the natural interest rate at the beginning of Chapter 2 highlighted that economies are likely to behave differently when official interest rates are at their effective lower bound than they do in normal times when the policy rate is above that floor. The Japanese experience during its two lost decades provides a good illustration of this, with two distinct regimes: a *disinflation regime*, with a declining but positive inflation rate (1992-1998); and a *deflationary regime* (1998-2012, except briefly in 2006-2008). The correlation of inflation, nominal and real interest rates was fundamentally different across these two regimes, as shown in the stylised representation of Figure 3.5.

Figure 3.5   Disinflation and deflation

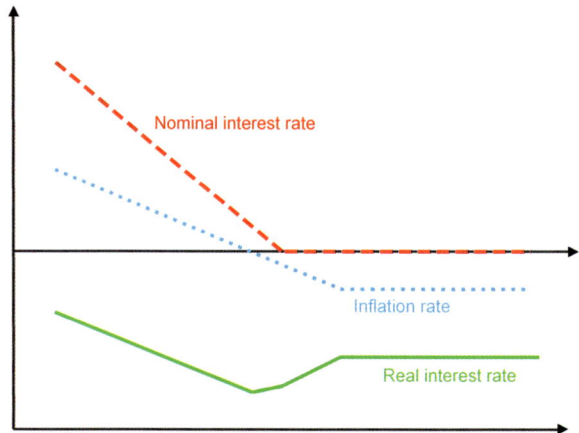

Within the disinflation regime, several factors appear to have restrained the growth of aggregate demand, including: financial distress after the bursting of the asset-price bubble; a tardy, and sometimes misguided, response by policymakers to the problems in the banking sector; monetary policy that was insufficiently resolute in maintaining a positive inflation rate; and premature monetary and fiscal tightening when it appeared that conditions were beginning to improve. The persistent weakness in aggregate demand accounts for both the decline in inflation and the fall – at a faster pace – in the interest rate. During this period, the inflation rate, the nominal interest rate and the real interest rate were positively correlated and all falling together.

The transition to the deflationary regime took place in 1998 after a severe recession took inflation into negative territory and led the Bank of Japan to cut its policy rate to nearly zero. At this point, the relationship between the inflation rate and the real interest rate changed. With further counter-cyclical cuts in interest rates no longer possible, the correlation between inflation and the real interest rate flipped sign, with further falls in inflation leading to a higher, rather than lower, real interest rate. That higher real interest rate in turn reinforced the weakness in aggregate demand and the downward pressure on prices, generating an adverse feedback loop. A *deflationary trap* thus developed, characterised by low growth, deflation and a zero nominal interest rate, with the real interest rate moving inversely to the inflation rate. Escaping such a trap requires either good luck (in the shape of an unexpected boost to aggregate demand) or bold policy measures. As it was, Japan remained mired in such a trap for the best part of 15 years.

3.2 From disinflation to deflation

Armed with this overview of the Japanese experience, we now provide a little more colour to developments as a prelude to our discussion of the authorities' responses and the associated lessons to be drawn.

The seeds of stagnation: The response to a bursting asset-price bubble

Japanese equity and real estate prices more than tripled during the latter half of the 1980s (Figure 3.6). On the back of higher collateral values, banks had lent to developers, construction companies and other businesses on the (mistaken) assumption that asset prices would continue to appreciate. The real estate boom, in particular, supported – and was in turn supported by – an expansion in credit to both companies and individuals.

Figure 3.6 Japanese equity and real-estate prices

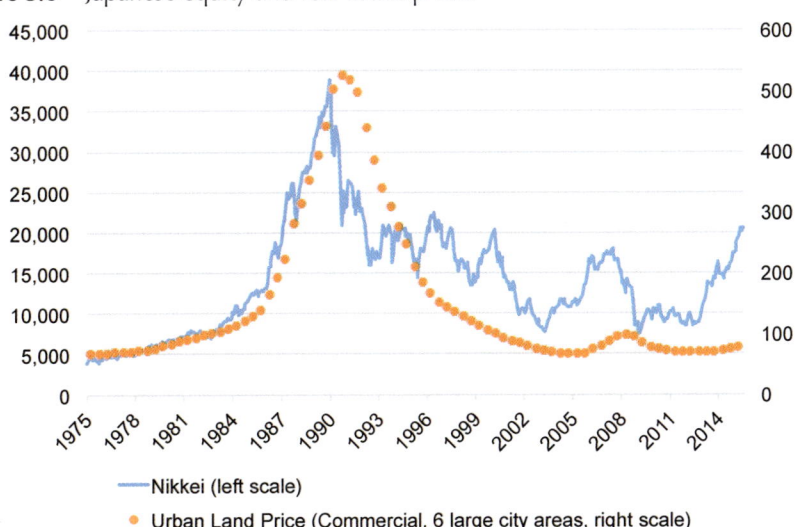

—— Nikkei (left scale)

● Urban Land Price (Commercial, 6 large city areas, right scale)

Source: Nikkei and Japan Real Estate Institute.

As the levels reached had become increasingly hard to rationalise in terms of expected future cash flows, the transition from rising to falling asset prices was initially welcomed by both policymakers and the public as necessary to bring asset – and especially real estate – prices back to affordable levels. Indeed, actions were taken to speed that adjustment: the policy rate was raised; a ceiling on lending to the real estate sector was implemented; a national land-holding tax was introduced; and capital gains tax was increased. Even though asset prices were already falling, it was thought important to kill off the bubble and clean up the excesses for good – the so-called 'cleansing view'. This was meant to provide the final nail in the coffin of the bubble economy.

With the benefit of hindsight, there were two problems with this approach. First, policymakers grossly underestimated the rising burden of non-performing loans on the banking system. As early as 1992, many developers found it impossible to maintain the payments on their bank loans. The banks, however, were willing to evergreen these non-performing loans, even though there was little prospect that they would eventually be repaid. Now a few real estate firms defaulting on their loans should not present the banks with any serious problem. But when many firms cannot repay, a systemic banking crisis is on the cards. Second, market participants had already switched from buying assets on the expectation of capital appreciation to selling them because prices were now expected to fall. No further nails were needed to make sure prices were moving back into line with fundamentals! Rather, there was a material risk that asset prices would undershoot.

The primary justification for the cleansing approach was that it would hasten a recovery by getting asset prices back into line with fundamentals sooner. But when the decline was reinforced by policy, the rapid fall in asset prices depressed both the economy and fundamentals, thus generating a pernicious feedback loop. That final nail in the coffin was a case of overkill.

The moral is that low, not high, interest rates are needed after an asset-price bubble bursts, especially when that bubble has been accompanied by a build-up in leverage. Asset-price falls need to be cushioned, while the health of bank balance sheets needs to be monitored closely with the aid of asset quality reviews and rigorous stress tests. That is a lesson that the Federal Reserve seems to have absorbed thoroughly in responding to the financial crisis of 2007-2008.

The banking crisis

From 1992 onwards, a growing number of smaller financial institutions failed, including credit cooperatives and mortgage companies (*jusen*). But significant disruption was not to come for several years, as Japanese banks had a huge cushion in the form of unrealised capital gains on equities held off balance sheet. This allowed them to delay dealing with their non-performing loans for too long, while banking supervisors also failed to exert enough pressure on the banks to clean up their balance sheets. Banks continued to lend to essentially insolvent 'zombie' firms, at the same time as they were restricting the supply of credit to new firms with better growth prospects.

In November 1997, Hokkaido Takushoku Bank (a large commercial bank), Yamaichi Securities (a large securities firm) and Sanyo Securities (a medium-sized securities firm) all failed. The failure of these firms was in many ways comparable in its impact to that of Lehman Brothers in 2008. When a large institution fails unexpectedly, it is apt to trigger distrust of other institutions as investors wonder who might be next in line. That was the case both in Japan in November 1997 and during the global financial panic in the autumn of 2008 (and, indeed, in numerous other systemic banking crises).

The failure of Hokkaido Takushoku Bank was particularly damaging to the stability of the financial system. Most people had assumed that such large banks were immune to failure – indeed, the finance minister had publicly said as much a few years earlier. Retail deposits were fully guaranteed, discouraging a conventional run by depositors. But the information on the state of bank balance sheets was increasingly regarded with suspicion by potential investors (including other banks). As a result, bank funding conditions began to deteriorate, with overseas banks demanding a substantial premium to lend to Japanese banks. This higher cost of funding forced the banks to shrink their balance sheets by offloading assets and restricting the supply of credit. As a consequence, investment fell sharply, pushing the economy into a period of very weak growth.

This crisis belatedly resulted in two rounds of bank recapitalisation. The first, in March 1998, must be deemed to have been something of a failure. The prior assessment of non-performing loans was not very rigorous, leading to only modest capital injections and insufficient differentiation across banks. Two more large banks failed later that year, a testimony to the inadequacy of the exercise. The scale of the subsequent capital injections in March 1999, though, was much larger, leading to a substantial increase in bank capital ratios.[6]

One key lesson from this episode is that the switch of policy regime from one of protecting all institutions to one of forcing failing banks into resolution or recapitalisation is only likely to succeed with the right legal and institutional framework. The supervisory agency needs a clear mandate to handle the problem of non-performing loans and insolvent financial institutions without political interference. The lack of an independent, transparent and credible bank recapitalisation only exacerbated the persistent disinflationary effects of the banking crisis.

The slide into deflation

Banking crises often have a large and prolonged adverse impact on economic activity, with output growth remaining depressed for a long time as households, companies and financial institutions seek to repair balance sheets (see, for example, Reinhart and Rogoff, 2009). Japan's experience after the 1997-1998 crisis was no exception, providing the impulse for a further weakening in aggregate demand and a slide into deflation.

The recession following the banking crisis also prompted important structural changes in the operation of the labour market. Large firms were forced to sack employees – something that was previously almost unheard of – leading labour unions to put a higher priority on job security than on securing higher wages. As a result, pay became more flexible downwards. Before 1998, Japanese companies

---

6   The story did not quite end here, as there was a further mini-crisis in 2002-2003. But on that occasion, the recapitalisation was prompt and based on a realistic assessment of balance-sheet health. By the end of 2003, the Japanese banking crisis could truly be declared over, a full decade after it began.

usually responded to a fall-off in demand by reducing bonuses. After 1998, it became more common to reduce base pay.

On the face of it, increased pay flexibility may seem like a good thing. But in a deflationary environment, it can have perverse consequences. In particular, it facilitated the establishment of a deflationary wage-price loop – wages fell because of expectations of deflation; lower wages resulted in lower consumption; and lower consumption increased the margin of economic slack. But once expectations of deflation had become entrenched, it became more difficult to stimulate activity.

3.3　Escaping the deflationary trap

Once Japan had slipped into deflation in 1998 and the Bank of Japan's policy rate had reached its effective floor, other policies were needed to provide additional stimulus. Policymakers do not have the luxury of making policy with hindsight, so, with little experience of dealing with deflation in a modern economy, it is hardly surprising that Japanese policymakers sometimes erred as they struggled to escape the deflationary trap. The discussion that follows is therefore offered in the spirit of learning from history, rather than meant as criticism.

3.3.1 Monetary policy

Japanese monetary policymakers seem to have taken several missteps during the two lost decades. These include: turning the bursting of the bubble into a hard landing in 1990-1992; failing to ease sufficiently early during the banking crisis of 1997-1998; a premature raising of the policy rate in 2000; insufficiently aggressive quantitative easing from 2001-2006, together with a reluctance to adopt a clear positive target for inflation; and too weak a response during the Great Recession, which resulted in a sharp appreciation of the yen.

Tightening into an asset-price bust, 1990-1992

As already discussed, the monetary tightening in 1990-1991 accentuated the sharp decline in real estate prices and stock prices that was already in train, so aggravating the downturn. It is worth remembering, though, that there was considerable public support for the policy because of its beneficial impact on the affordability of housing.

Tentative response to the 1997-1998 banking crisis

In 1998, the severe recession led inflation to slip into negative territory. But the monetary response was somewhat tentative, with the policy rate not reaching its lower bound – the zero interest rate policy (ZIRP) – until February of the following year. The Bank of Japan could perhaps also have been more vocal about the dangers of persistently falling prices and its intention to prevent deflation becoming entrenched. That might have helped to prevent inflation expectations following inflation down.

Premature policy tightening in 2000

When a ZIRP was introduced, the Bank of Japan declared that it would be maintained until "deflationary concerns are dispelled". The policy rate was, however, raised in August 2000, when prices were still falling. Moreover, the dot-com bubble was in the throes of bursting, also suggesting that more patience might have been prudent. The consequence of this premature increase in rates was that the Bank of Japan was seen as being more concerned about the consequences of keeping the policy rate at zero than preventing deflation.

Insufficiently aggressive application of quantitative easing in 2001-2006

Monetary policy was eased again in March 2001, when the Bank of Japan introduced an operating target for the quantity of bank reserves held on deposit at the central bank, implemented through an appropriate programme of open market asset purchases. Since banks' excess reserves were unremunerated, this also had the effect of pinning the interest rate in the interbank market to zero. In so doing, the Bank of Japan became the first central bank to embrace what is now known as quantitative easing (QE).

Unfortunately, the Bank did not communicate as clearly as it might have done the expected transmission channels, its ultimate inflation objective, and the conditions for exiting the policy. Several speeches by Policy Board members suggested that they lacked confidence in the efficacy of the policy in the prevailing environment. Moreover, market participants believed the Bank was not that troubled by deflation and was merely seeking to stop prices falling rather than return inflation to positive territory. The Bank could have tried to dispel such beliefs by following many other central banks in adopting an inflation target of, say, 2%. The Bank, however, argued that it would be very difficult to achieve such a target because deflationary expectations were already so entrenched, and that introducing such a target could damage the Bank's credibility if it failed to deliver. Consequently, the impact on agents' expectations fell short of what it might have been had the policy been pursued more wholeheartedly.

Nevertheless, both growth and inflation did pick up a little in 2003-2007, with a weaker yen adding to the stimulus. And, in July 2006, a few months after inflation had moved back into positive territory, the Bank decided it was appropriate to tighten policy a little, increasing the policy rate first to 0.25%,[7] with a further increase to 0.5% the following year.

---

7   Had there still been substantial unremunerated excess reserves in the system, the rise in the policy rate would have had a negligible impact on the marginal cost of bank funding and on market rate. However, the short maturity of the Bank's bond purchases meant that the quantity of excess reserves had already declined naturally to virtually zero by the time the policy rate was raised.

Response in the Great Recession

Like most other advanced economies, Japan suffered a large fall in output after the financial panic in the autumn of 2008. As a result, prices started to fall again, with deflation worsening in 2009. The economy was in danger of returning to the deflationary trap from which it had only recently escaped.

Figure 3.7   Balance sheets of major central banks (% of nominal GDP)

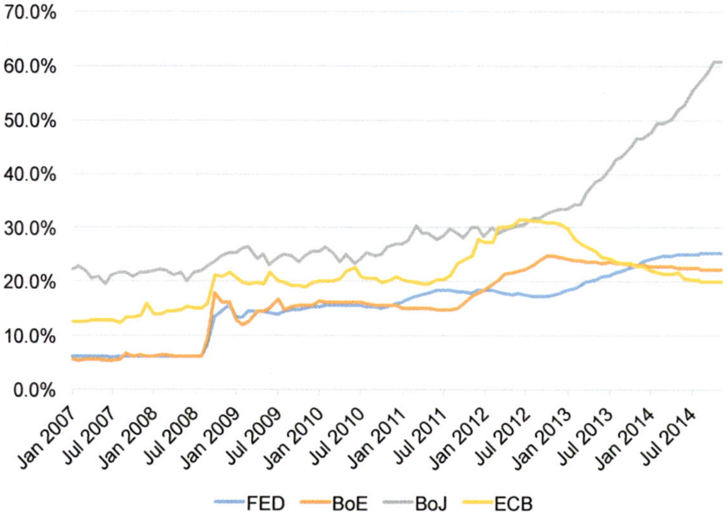

Source: Central bank websites.

While the Bank of Japan swiftly reverted to a ZIRP, it did not immediately follow the lead of the US Federal Reserve and the Bank of England in starting large-scale asset purchases (Figure 3.7 provides comparative data on the size of central bank balance sheets, relative to nominal GDP, since the crisis), nor was there the same need for the provision of extra liquidity assistance, as Japanese financial institutions were not directly affected by the turmoil in the western financial markets. Indeed, they took advantage of the crisis to acquire some of the troubled western institutions and assets cheaply. So it was reasonable to expect the impact of the western banking crisis on Japanese activity to be relatively modest. But this turned out to be mistaken. Although the linkage through international financial markets was not especially strong, there was powerful transmission through net exports as international trade collapsed. Moreover, in part perhaps reflecting the difference in monetary policy responses, the yen appreciated sharply, moving from 120 yen to the dollar to 80 yen to the dollar (Figure 3.8). That generated further downward pressure on both net exports and inflation. An earlier return to quantitative easing might have helped to dampen the downturn.

Figure 3.8   Dollar-yen exchange rate

Source: Bank of Japan.

3.3.2 Fiscal policy

When there is underutilisation of resources and the scope for monetary policy to stimulate demand is curtailed by the zero lower bound on interest rates, it is natural to look to fiscal policy to fill the gap. Indeed, the effectiveness of fiscal policy is potentially greater than in normal times, as any crowding out through upward pressure on the cost of debt finance is likely to be attenuated. So fiscal action is likely to be an effective response to a temporary, cyclical weakness in private sector demand.

When the private sector's contribution to aggregate demand is *persistently* weak, however, the output gap can only be closed if the government runs a *continuing* fiscal deficit. That in turn will lead the public debt to explode, ultimately resulting in either a debt crisis or high inflation if the debt is monetised. During the two lost decades, the Japanese government consistently ran a significant public deficit in order to try to offset the weakness in private demand. While our earlier discussion concluded that monetary policy was insufficiently resolute in its determination to end deflation, a similar charge cannot be levied at fiscal policy, despite several attempts at fiscal consolidation. The result was a substantial increase in government debt, with the ratio of gross public debt to GDP rising from around 65% in 1990 to 240% in 2012, though self-evidently that has not yet triggered a debt crisis.

Given these persistently high public deficits and rising public debts, it is no surprise that attention turned to fiscal consolidation whenever economic conditions appeared to be improving. In April 1997, the Hashimoto government raised VAT from 3% to 5%, ended a special income tax credit, and raised social security contributions. And, from 2001 to 2006, the Koizumi administration gradually shrank the deficit by capping expenditure and letting tax revenues rise with output.

The first of these episodes is of particular interest. All told, the fiscal contraction was equivalent to about 2% of GDP and led to an immediate downturn, though the economy returned to expansion in the next quarter. The longer-term effects are harder to isolate because of the banking crisis that broke towards the end of the year. There was a significant downturn in 1998, but how much of that was down to the fiscal consolidation and how much to the banking crisis is hard to disentangle. There are good reasons to think the latter was particularly important, but the impression lingered that fiscal consolidation was to blame for the 1998 recession. As a consequence, it subsequently became harder to justify embarking on fiscal consolidation.

With gross public debt now almost two and half times GDP, could a debt crisis happen in the near future, even though government bond yields remain at very low levels? After all, we saw during the Eurozone debt crisis that the dynamics of public debt can worsen dramatically once doubts arise over a sovereign's ability or willingness to honour its debts. There are a couple of counter-arguments worth rehearsing. First, Christian Broda and David Weinstein (2005) note that net government debt is substantially lower in Japan when calculated using standard international methods. Second, Takeo Hoshi and Takatoshi Ito (2013, 2014) argue that there is little immediate cause for concern, as 95% of Japanese government bonds are held by domestic entities, while there is also considerable room to raise VAT from its current relatively low rate of 8% should fiscal consolidation be required. Matters look less comforting a decade or so ahead, however, when the share of retirees in the population will be significantly higher. That has two implications for the public finances: higher social security (especially medical and pension) expenditures; and a reduced capacity for domestic saving to absorb government debt. So fiscal consolidation cannot be postponed too long.

3.3.3 Lessons

The Japanese experience shows how difficult it can be to escape durably from a deflationary trap when the policy rate is constrained by its lower bound. Counter-cyclical fiscal policies can provide a temporary respite, but on their own will not lead to a permanent solution. How much space there is for fiscal action will depend on: a realistic assessment of the future path of potential output; prospective fiscal burdens, such as those imposed by population ageing; and outstanding public debt. The margin for manoeuvre can be much smaller than it appears and narrows as the public debt rises. Moreover, running persistently large public deficits in order to sustain demand will lead the public debt to explode, with all the burdens and risks that entails; it is also prone to result in the misdirection of public spending.

Escaping a deflationary trap requires somehow shocking the economy out of its deflationary trap into a 'good' equilibrium, characterised by higher growth, modest positive inflation and interest rates that are clear of their lower bound. That is likely to require a combination of a credible and transparent treatment of non-performing loans, expansionary monetary policies to boost current activity and, depending on the outlook for future fiscal liabilities, possibly additional fiscal stimulus or temporary delays in fiscal consolidation. Despite the limits of zero rates, the central bank also needs to credibly communicate its intent not only to return the economy to a modestly positive rate of inflation but also to maintain it thereafter. Any fiscal stimulus can then be withdrawn and public debt stabilised as inflation and inflation expectations return to satisfactory levels and growth is restored. Specifically, incremental and half-hearted policies are not likely to be successful in generating such a jump from the deflationary trap back to a normal growth path with positive inflation. The strategy proposed and implemented by Shinzo Abe's government since its election in December 2012 embraces these ideas.

3.3.4 Abenomics

As noted above, the Great Recession left Japan suffering from an overly strong exchange rate, falling prices and stagnating output. And even though the policy rate was back at its floor, deflation meant the real interest rate was nevertheless in positive territory. By 2012, Japan had slipped back into a deflationary trap.

The economic programme of the new Abe government comprised three 'arrows': aggressive monetary expansion, together with an explicit target of 2% for core inflation; a temporary fiscal stimulus, to be followed by consolidation once growth picked up; and structural reforms to boost potential output. The intention was to bump the economy out of its deflationary trap into a 'good' equilibrium, characterised by higher growth, modest positive inflation and interest rates clear of their lower bound.

The monetary 'arrow', fired in April 2013 by Haruhiko Kuroda, the new Governor of the Bank of Japan, involved a commitment to double the monetary base over the following two years through purchases of Japanese government bonds and exchange-traded funds (see Figure 3.7). The programme also sought to lengthen the average maturity of the Bank of Japan's government bond purchases from three years to seven years. This dual aspect – increasing both size and duration – accounts for the programme being described as 'quantitative and qualitative easing' (QQE). The aim was to depress longer-term yields and drive up asset prices in general through portfolio rebalancing, thus boosting aggregate demand.

As it was, the mere expectation of more aggressive monetary expansion led to significant asset-price movements ahead of the formal announcement of the QQE programme. So, between the dissolution of the House of Representatives in November 2012 and the commencement of the programme, the yen depreciated by 15% and the Nikkei 225 stock price index rose by 40%. This is a striking example of the impact that the mere expectation of a change in policy can have. Moreover, the scale of the QQE programme when it was announced exceeded market expectation, leading to further yen depreciation and equity price increases. This correction of the previously overvalued yen represented a notable achievement of the policy.

Turning to the fiscal 'arrow', shortly after taking office the new government introduced a supplementary fiscal package worth 10 trillion yen. This was focused on public investment for disaster prevention and reconstruction, together with measures to boost private investment. The package was projected to boost GDP by a hefty 2%.

The immediate results from the new monetary and fiscal policies were encouraging: growth picked up and inflation rose. Thoughts then turned to the necessary medium-term fiscal consolidation, with the government legislating for an increase in VAT in April 2014. Though the timing of this switch from fiscal expansion to consolidation was controversial, by April 2014 the economic indicators were looking favourable and the hope was that any adverse impact of the tax hike on growth would prove short-lived. In the event, the impact turned out to be greater and more persistent than expected, producing a renewed downturn and leading inflation to fall back again.

In response, the Bank of Japan resolved to increase the pace of asset purchases, while the government announced that a second scheduled hike in consumption taxes would be postponed by 18 months. With an additional stimulus coming from lower oil prices, the economy finally started to grow again in the first quarter of this year, while underlying inflation also began to rise – excluding oil, the inflation rate is presently around 0.7%.

Thus far, the new strategy to escape deflation seems to have been reasonably successful. Prices are rising rather than falling, the yen is well off of its extreme highs and there is moderate growth. For now, at least, the deflationary trap seems to have been consigned to history. But the job is only half done, as the economy is not yet set on a durably higher growth path. And achieving that requires resolute implementation of the third 'arrow' of structural reform and liberalisation. Without that third arrow, not only will growth suffer, but the necessary longer-term fiscal consolidation will also prove more challenging.

3.3.5 Avoiding deflation: A summing-up

Here are some of the lessons from Japan's 'two lost decades':
*   Prevention is better than cure – it is best not to let an asset-price bubble form in the first place! Moreover, bubbles supported by increased leverage – as is the case with most real estate bubbles – are particularly dangerous. But once a bubble starts to unwind, it is better to moderate, rather than accelerate, the correction.
*   The problem of non-performing loans needs to be tackled promptly, even though banks may prefer to evergreen such loans in order to make their balance sheets look healthier. Getting the banking system back on its feet quickly requires the rigorous evaluation of bank balance sheets together with any necessary bank recapitalisation. Not doing so is only likely to lead to a worse banking crisis in the future.
*   Monetary policy needs to be especially stimulatory if there is a material risk of getting trapped in deflation. When policy rates reach their lower bound, the real interest rate starts to behave pro-cyclically, amplifying the weakness in demand.

- Fiscal policy should be strongly counter-cyclical when policy rates are constrained by their lower bound, provided that there is sufficient room for manoeuvre, bearing in mind the prospective path for output, the outlook for future fiscal liabilities and the existing level of public debt. That also means governments should try to create more fiscal space when they have the opportunity to do so.
- It is better to prevent deflation in the first place. But if it does occur, the central bank must not allow it to become ingrained into inflation expectations. An early and resolute monetary policy response can help to prevent that.

3.4   Effects of low interest rates on the private sector

An environment of persistently low interest rates poses special challenges not only for policymakers but also for private sector investors, both institutional and retail. As far as the former goes, many life insurance companies had sold products that guaranteed a minimum return in the event of paying out. But if the returns on the investments that back those products declines, the margin the company earns on them will obviously decline. Either institutions accept this – which may imply the business becomes unprofitable – or else they try to raise returns by shifting into higher-yielding but riskier assets in the hope of generating the profits necessary to meet the expected pay outs (we return to this issue in Chapter 4). Either way, the likelihood of failure rises. Between 1997 and 2000, seven life insurance companies failed, though the wider consequences of these failures turned out to be relatively limited.

The very low interest rates available on Japanese assets also encouraged investors to take advantage of the higher returns available overseas. But holding assets denominated in another currency also exposes the investor to foreign currency risk: if the home currency appreciates (depreciates), then the investor suffers a loss (gain). The difference in (expected) rates of return should therefore reflect any expectation of exchange rate changes. Many investors behaved, however, as though yen exchange rate appreciation was unlikely (or they could liquidate their foreign currency positions before such appreciation occurred). Moreover, not only did investors purchase foreign assets, many of them also borrowed in yen in order to do so, with the result that investor net worth became more sensitive to exchange rate movements. Some estimates suggest that, on the eve of the financial crisis, as much as one trillion dollars had been staked on this so-called yen carry trade.

Moreover, it was not just professional investors that engaged in purchases of foreign bonds. Some retail investors – particularly pensioner households (the proverbial 'Mrs Watanabe') – look to their savings to provide a steady income flow, making bonds an attractive vehicle. The low returns available on domestic bonds led some of those households to seek higher returns by investing in foreign bonds, particularly those of the emerging economies and trust funds invested in such bonds. Some of these retail investors were also financing their investments by borrowing in domestic currency, just like their professional counterparts, though almost certainly with less understanding of the currency and credit risks they were thereby exposed to.

3.5   Demography

The Japanese experience is also potentially instructive along another dimension. In Chapter 2, we argued that population ageing was an important contributory factor to the decline in the neutral real interest rate since the late 1990s. That force should, however, start working in the other direction as the present bulge of high-saving older workers moves through into retirement and begins to dissave. But demographic trends in Japan have been running ahead of those elsewhere: the population has been shrinking since 2007, while the population share of the middle-aged (40-65 years) has been falling since the mid-1990s. Is there any sign that this has been associated with a declining aggregate saving rate?

Our discussion in Chapter 2 suggested that the relevant indicator to capture demographic pressures on the aggregate household savings rate is the difference in the respective population shares of the high-saving middle-aged and of the dissaving retirees. Figure 3.9 shows the same indicator that we employed earlier (see Figure 2.4) for Japan; it peaked in the early 1990s and has been falling back steadily since. The figure appears to suggest that the savings rate, which peaked in the mid-1970s, turned down before the demographic indicator. This is misleading, however, as the rise in the savings rate in the 1970s probably reflects the need to increase saving to preserve the real value of nominally denominated assets in the face of the spike in inflation (and nominal interest rates) after the first oil price shock. What is more notable is the decline in the savings rate from double-digit levels in the late 1980s to around 1% now. This certainly appears consistent with a strong impact from ageing.

Of course, as noted above, savings is not the only thing affected by an ageing population. Fiscal deficits tend to worsen as pension and health care spending rise and income tax revenues suffer as the share of the population working shrinks. Slower labour-force growth also implies that potential output slows and that less investment is required to maintain the capital-labour ratio (though businesses may respond to the shortage of workers by raising the capital intensity of production). So the net impact on the balance between aggregate savings and investment is quite complex.[8]

---

8   It follows that the impact of demography on the balance between aggregate demand and supply is equally complex. It would be a mistake, however, to shift the blame for Japan's disinflation and deflation onto demographic developments, as some have sought to do. Rather, it represents a failure by the central bank to ensure that monetary conditions were appropriately adjusted in the face of those developments so as to maintain the right balance between demand and supply, and thus stabilising inflation. Demography is a real economic phenomenon, but inflation is ultimately a monetary one.

Figure 3.9   Demographic pressures and household saving in Japan

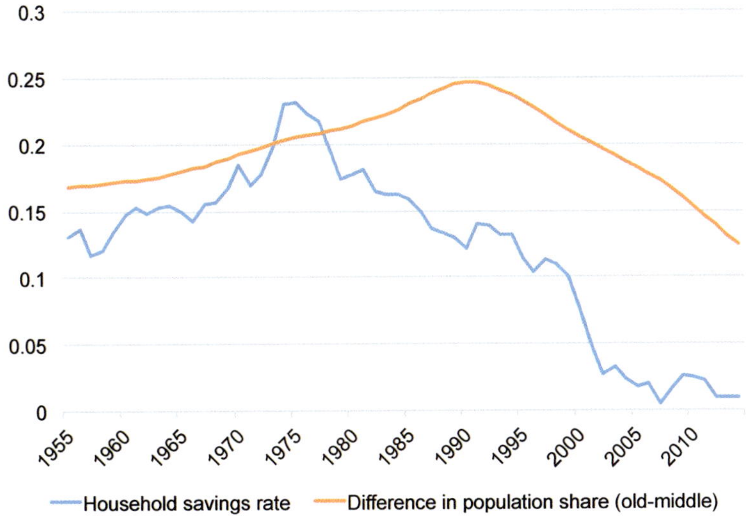

Source: United Nations and Statistics Japan.

Figure 3.3 shows that real interest rates have been broadly flat (though with significant cyclical fluctuations) over the past two decades. That might appear to imply that the various demographic effects have roughly netted out in terms of their impact on interest rates. Such a conclusion is unwarranted. First, for most of this period policy rates have been at the effective floor. As we noted at the beginning of Chapter 2, in such circumstances the natural rate of interest is not observed and must lie beneath the observed rate. Second, given the high degree of financial integration, the natural real rate of interest will be determined primarily by global rather than local forces. Third, at least at the end of the period, longer-term yields are likely to have been depressed by the Bank of Japan's asset purchases. Consequently, not much can be concluded about the link between demographics and the natural real interest rate from the behaviour of Japanese interest rates alone over this period.

4 Policies and prospects

The final chapter of this report explores some of the consequences should the natural, or equilibrium, real rate of interest remain at unusually low levels. We start by looking at the implications for monetary policy. As our discussion of Japan's 'two lost decades' brought out, the (near) zero lower bound on interest rates greatly complicates the conduct of policy and heightens the risk that an economy may get caught in a deflationary trap. In such circumstances, the central bank needs to turn to unconventional monetary instruments. How effective are these and can anything be done to alleviate the lower bound constraint?

We then turn to a consideration of the impact of low interest rates on the behaviour of participants in the financial markets. Again, the Japanese experience suggests that an environment of persistently low interest rates can have some significant, and potentially unwanted, effects that heighten the risk of financial instability. Since the financial crisis, there has been increased interest in the use of prudential and regulatory policies to contain and mitigate financial stability risks. Are these up to the challenge?

To conclude, we turn to the outlook for longer-term interest rates. Chapter 2 examined the possible drivers of the decline in the underlying risk-free real rate of interest since the late 1990s. We concluded there that demographics and Chinese financial integration had probably played a part, particularly in the years before the financial crisis. And since then, heightened risk aversion is likely both to have inhibited investment and led to a higher relative demand for safe assets, thus depressing the yield on them relative to that available on riskier assets. But how will these and other drivers of the natural safe real rate of interest evolve in the future, and how might they be affected by policy choices?

4.1 Monetary policy

As noted in Chapter 1, absent cost shocks, the optimal monetary policy will normally require setting the policy rate equal to the natural or Wicksellian nominal rate of interest. In turn, that rate is just the sum of the natural real rate, determined by the balance between savings and investment, and the central bank's target rate of inflation. We address the question of the appropriate inflation target later, but for now treat that as given. Then the most obvious consequence of a persistently low natural real rate is that the zero lower bound on interest rates is more likely to constrain the central bank's choices.

The experience of Japan illustrates the importance of preventing the economy being sucked into a deflationary trap. Once in such a trap, it can be hard to escape. Wen the interest rate is pinned to its floor, deflation increases the real interest rate and raises the burden of debt. That can lead to a debt-deflation spiral, where higher debt burdens and higher real interest rates lead to more bankruptcies and less investment, putting further downward pressure on activity. And, as mentioned in Chapter 3, it can also generate a downward spiral in pay and consumer demand. So aggressive action by the central bank to prevent such an outcome is most certainly warranted. But how effective can monetary policy be in this environment?

To begin, it is clear that the zero lower bound does not apply strictly; for instance, the European, Danish and Swiss central banks are already charging banks to hold reserves on deposit. The source of the zero lower bound constraint lies in the unrestricted convertibility into cash of reserve accounts at the central bank. In practice, however, banks do not immediately cash in their reserve balances as soon as they are charged for holding them, because carrying large volumes of cash represents a significant security risk. So a bank would need to be able to provide sufficiently secure storage space in which to hold the cash. This is not a trivial issue, but banks are more likely to decide that it will be worth investing in setting up such secure facilities if central bank deposit rates are likely to be negative frequently and for substantial periods. Some illustrative calculations carried out by the Bank of England (2013) suggested that such substitution from reserves to cash might begin to occur if central bank deposit rates were persistently -0.5% or lower. So the true floor is probably somewhere in that region.

It is worth noting, however, that other nominal rigidities may lead a central bank to conclude that the *effective* floor for policy rates is above its formal lower bound. For example, in 2009 during the Great Recession, the Bank of England's Monetary Policy Committee decided not to lower its official policy rate below +0.5%. That decision reflected specific rigidities operating in UK financial markets. In particular, many mortgages were (and still are) contractually linked to the policy rate, while UK banks and building societies conventionally do not charge for current account services. Further reductions in the policy rate would have squeezed mortgage-bank profit margins enough to have threatened their stability as well as their ability to extend new credit, thus raising the possibility of a perverse effect on aggregate demand from further rate cuts. Of course, these should just be transitory impediments that disappear once conventions about the pricing of deposit accounts change and the mortgage book is re-priced. But such frictional considerations can nevertheless be of practical relevance.

Leaving the niceties of whether the lower bound on policy rates is zero, a small negative number or a small positive number to one side, how much difference does it make? Around the turn of the millennium, following Japan's lost decade, but before the trend decline in global real interest rates was properly appreciated, several authors undertook assessments of the impact of the zero lower bound on the conduct of monetary policy. For instance, simulating the Federal Reserve Board's macroeconomic model, David Reifschneider and John Williams (2000) found that, under a standard Taylor rule, with a natural real rate of interest averaging 2½% and a 2% inflation target, the zero lower bound would bind about 5% of the time and that such episodes would on average last just a year. But with an inflation target of zero, the zero lower bound would bind almost 15% of the time and the mean duration of zero lower bound episodes rose to six quarters.

From an analytic perspective, a two percentage-point reduction in the inflation target is the equivalent of a two percentage-point reduction in the natural real rate of interest. And that is the order of the likely fall in the future long-term real rate relative to the historical experience. So this experiment also provides us with an assessment of how much more frequent and longer-lasting zero lower bound episodes are likely to be.

This calculation if anything understates the likely increase in frequency, severity and duration of zero lower bound episodes under the 'new normal'. Exercises like that of Reifschneider and Williams have usually been calibrated on the basis of pre-crisis economic volatility.[9] The collapse in aggregate demand during the Great Recession meant that policy rates of the order of -5% would have been warranted on the basis of the Taylor rule (see Rudebusch, 2009). Moreover, policy rates have been at, or close to, their effective lower bound for six years, far longer than the mean duration in the Reifschneider and Williams exercise. While the 2007-2008 financial crisis is hopefully a once-in-a-century event, with hindsight the years of the Great Moderation seem equally abnormal. The zero lower bound can no longer be treated as a curiosum.

Central banks are, however, not completely out of monetary ammunition once the zero lower bound is reached. In particular, they can still influence the level of demand by influencing agents' expectations of the future path of policy rates through forward guidance. And they can alter term premia and asset prices through large-scale asset purchases – so-called quantitative easing. Finally, suitably targeted lending policies can also raise the supply of credit.

In academic analyses, such as that of Mike Woodford (2012), forward guidance works through influencing private-sector expectations of future policy rates and inflation, which in many settings will feed back to affect activity today. In particular, a commitment to hold policy rates at the zero lower bound *past* the point at which rates would normally have begun to rise will generate a future boom with excess inflation, which – at least in the standard model – raises output today (e.g. by lowering the long-term real interest rate). Such a policy is, however, time-inconsistent: once the emergency is over, the central bank has no incentive to deliver on its past promise to generate an inflationary boom. Moreover, it is difficult to see how such a commitment can be implemented in practice. Central bankers cannot tie the hands of their successors, so such promises are only credible for a short period ahead. In any case, in practice central banks' forward guidance largely seems to have been directed more towards the provision of better communication of their reaction function than the implementation of a time-inconsistent policy path (for some evidence on this, see Moessner et al. 2015).

Turning to quantitative easing, all four of the major central banks have, or are, engaged in large-scale asset purchases. The transmission mechanism of such purchases potentially operates through three channels: a bank liquidity channel,

---

9   Analyses of the zero lower bound problem since the crisis recognise this; see, for example, Williams (2014).

whereby an increase in bank reserves results in an expansion in credit supply; a portfolio rebalancing channel, whereby the re-investment of the proceeds from the asset sales into substitute assets results in a generalised rise in asset prices; and a signalling channel, whereby asset purchases reinforce expectations that policy will remain accommodative. The Japanese experience suggests that the first channel is likely to be weak after a financial crisis, something that has been largely borne out in the other jurisdictions since. That leaves the portfolio rebalancing and signalling channels as the main routes whereby asset purchases by the central bank can boost activity.

There are theoretical reasons why the asset purchases could have proved ineffective. In particular, Gauti Eggerston and Mike Woodford (2003) show that once the zero lower bound has been reached and the value of extra liquidity has fallen to zero, central bank asset purchases should be neutral in their effect on the real economy. That is because, at least in the environment they study, private agents can always exactly undo the consequences for the subsequent path of the public finances of the balance sheet change.

Be that as it may, event studies on both sides of the Atlantic suggest that central bank asset purchases *have* been effective at lowering longer-term interest rates and raising asset prices. For instance, the studies by Joe Gagnon, Matthew Raskin, Julie Remache, and Brian Sack (2010) and Arvind Krishnamurthy and Annette Vissing-Jorgensen (2011) found that the US Federal Reserve's $1.75 trillion programme of asset purchases during 2008-2009 ('QE1') lowered long-term Treasury yields by around a percentage point. And research by Mike Joyce, Ana Lasaosa, Ibrahim Stevens and Matt Tong (2011) for the Bank of England's programme of £200 billion asset purchases during 2009-2010 (also commonly referred to as 'QE1') found an effect of broadly the same magnitude on UK gilt yields from what – relative to size of the economy – was a similar quantum of purchases to that of the Federal Reserve.

Event studies of the subsequent asset purchase programmes generally find somewhat smaller effects (see, for example, Krishnamurthy and Vissing-Jorgenson, 2013). In part, that may be because, unlike the QE1 programmes, their introduction was in part anticipated and so already discounted into asset prices. And that has certainly been the case with the ECB's recently instituted €60 billion/month bond purchase programme. That said, there are several reasons to think that the efficacy of asset purchases is likely to be lower when markets are functioning normally than when they are dysfunctional, as was the case in the months after the collapse of Lehman Brothers.

In addition, there are several reasons why the continued application of monetary stimulus through asset purchases might display diminishing returns.[10] First, a flatter yield curve reduces the incentive for banks to undertake maturity transformation. Moreover, although the expansion in bank reserves associated with asset purchases may not have greatly stimulated the supply of credit, it nevertheless helped banks to recapitalise by generating increases in asset values.

---

10 Though as Bernanke (2015) notes, "with short-term interest rates pinned near zero, monetary policy is not as powerful or as predictable as at other times.... the right inference is not that we should stop using monetary policy, but rather that we should bring to bear other policy tools as well."

That effect is likely to become quantitatively less significant as the yield curve flattens.

Second, large-scale asset purchases take a central bank increasingly into political territory. The more – and the more regularly – the central bank buys public debt, the more private agents may suspect that they are taking place at the behest of government rather than for monetary policy purposes. The economy may thus slide into an equilibrium characterised by fiscal, rather than monetary, dominance. One might then see the inflation premium on nominal sovereign debt rising.

The central bank can avoid that by buying private securities instead of public securities. But that brings other problems. If the central bank buys private credit instruments, it is exposing the public sector finances to the risk of credit losses, which is unlikely to go down well with the politicians. Moreover, those same politicians will, quite reasonably, want to have a say in which assets are bought (e.g. small business credits or favoured sectors of industry). And if the central bank buys equities, it amounts to a form of quasi-nationalisation. There may be ways to deal with this, for instance holding them in a separately managed sovereign wealth fund. But the basic point that consistent use of large-scale asset purchases can blur the line between monetary and fiscal activities still stands.

Finally, we have seen on several occasions in the past few years that quantitative easing can generate international tensions through its impact on exchange rates – the 'currency wars' charge of former Brazilian Finance Minister Guido Mantega – and on international flows of capital. One of the transmission channels of conventional expansionary monetary policy is through depreciating the exchange rate. But the impact of that on trading partners is offset by the countervailing increase in imports generated by higher domestic demand. When that expansion takes place through asset purchases, the latter effect can seem less apparent to other countries, especially when normal transmission channels through the banking system are impaired, as has been the case in the past few years. Moreover, even when these countervailing demand effects are recognised, other countries are still faced with managing the consequential inflows and outflows of capital. For emerging economies, these flows can create financial stability risks if they generate currency and maturity mismatches on the balance sheets of financial institutions, businesses and households.

Given these limitations, it is natural, therefore, to ask whether there are ways of restoring the efficacy of conventional monetary policy, or at least reducing the zone within which the zero lower bound binds. One seemingly obvious response is to follow the suggestion of Olivier Blanchard, Giovanni Dell'Ariccia and Paolo Mauro (2010) and raise central bank inflation targets from their current levels of around 2% to, say, 4%, providing an extra two percentage points of room for manoeuvre. Indeed, doing so may seem pretty much a no-brainer.

There are, though, three counter-arguments that should be considered. First, 2% inflation is close enough to price stability – especially when the difficulties of measuring quality improvements are taken into account – that households and businesses can for many purposes effectively ignore it. That is not really the case at 4% inflation, even though the two percentage-point rise might appear rather modest. While it may not figure in economists' models, there is probably considerable social value in people being able to follow the simple heuristic that the average price level is broadly constant. Moreover, given the positive association between levels and variability of inflation, the regime would probably not anchor expectations so well.

Second, even though it might have proved helpful if inflation targets had been a little higher at the outset of the crisis, raising them now when central banks have been struggling even to meet their current targets is hardly conducive to maintaining credibility.

Finally, an increase in the inflation target could also engender expectations that fiscally challenged governments might be tempted to press for even higher inflation in order to inflate away the real value of nominally denominated debt. That, in turn, would be likely to generate an unhelpful rise in the inflation risk premium.

In principle, one can also attack things from the other side by seeking to relax the zero lower bound constraint itself. One approach is to get rid of cash altogether, so making it impossible for banks to avoid charges on their reserve holdings by substitution. The increased use of cashless payment technologies has made this a more practical option than it was, but one needs to recognise that cash is still an extremely convenient medium for undertaking transactions that are modest in size.

An alternative is to charge interest on cash holdings as well as reserves, an idea advanced a century ago by Silvio Gesell (1916). This could be achieved by requiring that bank notes be periodically stamped (at a charge) in order to remain valid, or else by declaring that notes with a serial number ending in a randomly chosen digit have ceased to be legal tender.

Finally, Willem Buiter (2009) has revived an idea originally due to Robert Eisler (1932). This involves decoupling the numéraire from the medium of exchange and implementing a variable rate of exchange between them.[11] As the choice of numéraire is ultimately a matter of choice for society rather than government, this cannot be done by diktat. Breaking the one-for-one exchange rate between cash and reserves, so that the price of cash relative to reserves falls over time,[12] could, however, achieve the same outcome.

Most of these solutions seem somewhat exotic at the current juncture, though were present conditions to persist indefinitely, then they might start to look more attractive. But in our view, finding a way to loosen the constraint imposed by the zero lower bound is not the most important of the policy challenges facing central banks in a world of persistently low real interest rates. Rather it is the increased risk of financial instability. And making possible even lower interest rates by lessening or removing the zero lower bound constraint potentially simply serves to increase this risk.

---

11   Tyler Cowen and Randall Kroszner (1994) provide a general discussion of these and related issues.
12   A strategy of switching reserves into cash for a period to avoid the interest charge on the former and then switching back thus incurs an offsetting capital loss.

4.2 Financial markets and financial stability

A persistently low natural real rate of interest is thus likely to raise the frequency and duration of episodes when policy rates are at their lower bound and lead to increased reliance on unconventional monetary policies to stabilise inflation and activity instead. But, as we have seen, the more those policies are deployed, the less effective and the more problematic they may turn out to be. But this is not the only – or perhaps even the most important – consequence of a persistently low natural real rate. There are likely to be other effects on financial markets, with possible implications for financial stability.

In particular, some commentators have suggested that long periods of low interest rates are apt to result in a leveraged 'reach for yield', excessive risk-taking and asset-price bubbles (e.g. Bank for International Settlements, 2015; Stein, 2013). There are a variety of mechanisms that might result in such behaviour.

First, an environment of persistently low interest rates favours debt-financed investment in long-lived assets, such as housing, that are highly leveraged. While that is entirely rational, an economy in which households and businesses are indebted does tend to be more vulnerable to shocks than one which is less highly levered (see, for instance, Figure 2.9). It is worth remembering, however, that a low interest rate environment should also help households and businesses that are already encumbered by high debt to reduce their indebtedness. So whether persistently low interest rates lead to higher or lower indebtedness depends on the balance of these two forces.

Second, a low real rate of return on safe assets makes it more expensive to accumulate the savings necessary to provide for retirement. As a result, households will be tempted to look for ways to build savings other than investing in bond-heavy pension funds. If the funds flow into the stock market, lowering the cost of capital and boosting productive investment, then that would not matter. But past experience suggests that such funds often flow into real estate instead. And, if mortgage rates remain low, it will be tempting for households to try to lever up the returns from investment in property by increasing their borrowing. An expansion in buy-to-let property investment and further upward pressure on house prices reflecting the relative attractiveness of property as an investment asset therefore seems an entirely plausible outcome.

Third, during the earlier period of higher interest rates, many pension funds and insurance companies will have sold products that offer guaranteed returns over long horizons. This will not matter if the institutions have matched the maturity and risk profile of their investments against their obligations. But to the extent that these long-term obligations have been incompletely matched, they may face the prospect of making losses on these products. For instance, suppose the assets are safe but of shorter maturity than the corresponding obligations. In that case, they can reinvest the maturing assets in new safe securities, thereby crystallising the losses. Alternatively, they may be tempted to 'reach for yield' by purchasing risky securities offering higher expected yields; this gamble pays off if returns are high, but of course also opens the institution to the risk of incurring even higher future losses.

Fourth, there may be nominal rigidities arising from accounting practices and remuneration practices that can also induce a 'reach for yield'. For instance, asset managers and hedge funds are often judged on their performance relative to benchmarks that may only adjust slowly to the new low-rate environment. Again that may lead to a 'reach for yield', possibly magnified by the use of leverage, in order to try to maintain returns. Moreover, investors are likely to be loath to pay significant fees for nugatory returns (many hedge funds have been accustomed to charging 2% of the sum invested and 20% of the returns). Consequently some business models will no longer be viable unless returns can somehow be levered up.

So a persistently low interest rate may lead to higher indebtedness and a leveraged 'reach for yield'. In turn, that increases the vulnerability of the economy to future shocks and may also increase the risk of future financial instability. Indeed, there is a view that such behaviour can lead to serial financial boom-busts (see Box 4.1).

In case it seems premature to be worrying about such risks when there is still significant underutilisation of resources and negligible inflation, it is worth noting the recent strong growth in the leveraged finance of US corporates. Figure 4.1 provides information on the issuance of leveraged loans and high-yield bonds; in each of the past three years this has exceeded the levels seen immediately before the crisis. Figure 4.2 gives data on the amount outstanding of cov-lite and second-lien loans – the riskiest segments – which have quadrupled over the past couple of years. This suggests that financial risks can build even though activity may not be robust.

Furthermore, as mentioned in Chapter 2 – and extensively documented by authors such as Carmen Reinhart and Kenneth Rogoff (2010); Moritz Schularick and Alan Taylor (2012); Atif Mian and Amir Sufi (2014); and Luigi Buttiglione, Philip Lane, Lucrezia Reichlin and Vincent Reinhart (2014) – excessive leverage is also a prime cause of slow growth in the wake of such crises. If debt is already high and higher demand today can only be achieved by stimulating the further accumulation of debt, then it may also increase the likelihood of low growth and deflationary outcomes tomorrow. In such circumstances, the policymaker therefore faces an intertemporal trade-off: generating higher activity today may lead to lower activity tomorrow. To a degree, that is always true for monetary policy, as changes in interest rates are meant to elicit the intertemporal substitution of spending. But the trade-off is harder to handle when recessions are persistent rather than short-lived and the future adverse consequences from expansionary policy today may be large.

Figure 4.1   Issuance of leveraged loans and high-yield bonds

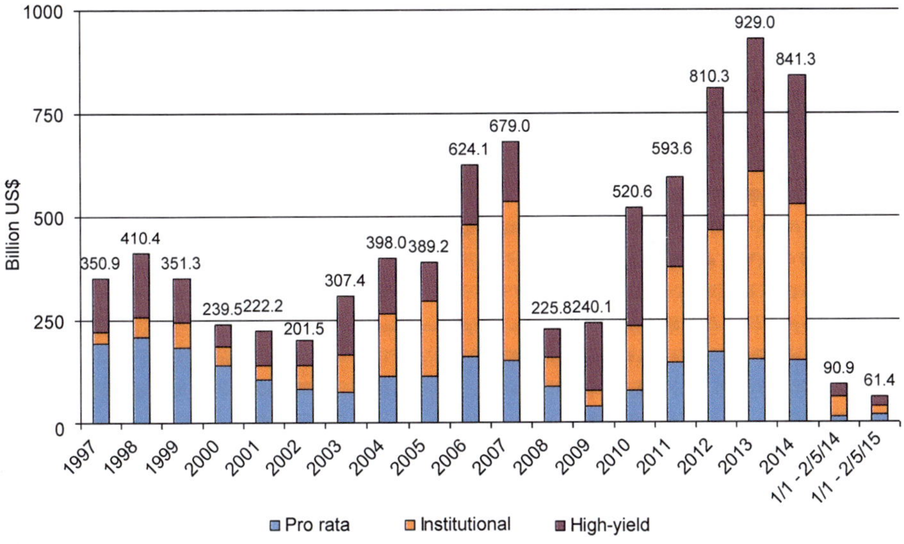

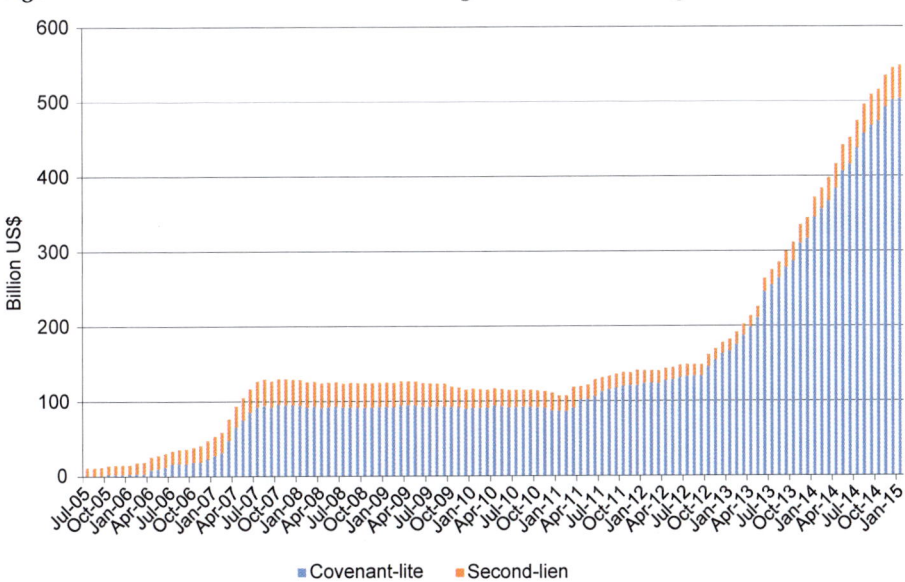

Source: Standard and Poor's.

Figure 4.2   Cov-lite and second-lien leveraged loans outstanding

Source: Standard and Poor's.

Box 4.1   Serial financial crises

One interpretation of 2007-2008 is that it was a once-in-a-century event, in which several factors came together to create the pre-conditions for a particularly severe financial crisis and a subsequent deep and persistent downturn. A by no means exhaustive list would include: low short- and long-term interest rates; an insouciance to risk borne of the Great Moderation; financial engineering that was supposed to have spread risk but ended up concentrating it; remuneration schemes that distorted behaviour; opacity of exposures to risk; fragile bank funding models; excessively thin bank capital buffers; and inadequate mechanisms for handling failing systemically important financial institutions. Together, these encouraged a rise in the leverage of financial institutions and of households and a mistaken belief on the part of both participants and regulators that the system was safer than it in fact was. Seen from this perspective, addressing those failings and ensuring that the lessons are not forgotten should help to ensure the experience is not repeated.

A more pessimistic view is, however, possible: we may be locked into a recurring cycle of financial crises. This view, deriving from the writings of Hyman Minsky, runs as follows. During the boom phase of the cycle, excessive optimism leads to an (over-)accumulation of assets (either physical capital or real estate) financed by credit expansion. Something then happens to puncture that over-optimism, revealing the underlying fragilities and a collapse in demand as highly indebted agents seek to de-lever. As a result, the natural or Wicksellian real interest rate falls, in turn prompting a relaxation in the monetary stance. But if the previous boom had been associated with over-investment, then even very loose monetary policy may be ineffective in stimulating investment. So the sensitivity of aggregate demand to interest rates falls and policy will need to remain stimulatory until the excess investment is worked off.

In this interpretation, the persistently low interest rate is prone to encourage a leveraged search for yield, manifested in the first instance by increases in the price of existing assets rather than investment in new assets. So asset prices rise, even though consumer price inflation remains subdued. The risk is that the former evolves into an asset-price bubble, where demand is driven by expectations of capital gains, before the central bank is prompted to tighten policy by rising inflation pressures. When the central bank finally starts tightening, it risks prompting the bubble to collapse, so starting the next cycle. Put simply, another bubble is needed to alleviate the aftermath of the previous bubble. Moreover, this cycle will be amplified when bank capital buffers are thin. If such a characterisation is appropriate, central banks and prudential regulators therefore need to be particularly awake to incipient financial stability risks even quite early in the recovery phase.

The bottom line from all this is that the risk-return trade-off confronting central banks deteriorates when the natural real rate of interest falls to low levels. In normal circumstances and absent cost shocks, optimal policy, as embodied in flexible inflation targeting regimes, requires keeping the policy rate in line with its natural level (the natural real rate of interest plus the inflation target). But the increased likelihood of financial stability risks at low natural real rates means that it is no longer appropriate to keep the policy rate in line with its natural level, unless those risks can somehow be dealt with through other policies.

The post-crisis conventional wisdom is that financial stability risks should in the first instance be managed through the use of prudential policies. These include both systemic changes that boost financial sector resilience, such as enhanced bank-capital standards that deliver greater capacity to absorb losses, and selective macroprudential interventions that discourage risky or excessive credit expansion. Such prioritisation involves the allocation of instruments to the task to which they are best suited: monetary policy to maintaining aggregate demand at a level consistent with price stability, and prudential policies to mitigating financial stability risks.

What sorts of policies might be appropriate for dealing with the potential consequences of a low-rate environment that we discussed earlier? First, in some countries the tax system accords a privileged status to debt, for example, through the tax deductibility of interest payments or assistance for those taking out a home mortgage. So if the primary concern is that persistently low interest rates encourage excessive debt accumulation, eliminating this privileged treatment would seem sensible.

Second, if low rates are promoting a general frothiness in parts of the financial sector, then various macroprudential tools may help to inhibit the build-up of leverage and prevent dangerous asset-price dislocations. For instance, if the problems are concentrated in the real estate sector, several options are available. Forcing banks to hold more capital against residential mortgages by increasing the associated risk-weight would both increase resilience and inhibit the supply of mortgage finance. Increasing down-payment requirements or restricting the share of high loan-to-income mortgages are alternative ways of restricting mortgage availability.

Third, if factors such as balance-sheet mismatches are driving a 'reach for yield', then regulation and supervision of the institutions concerned needs to play a central role. More generally, regulators and supervisors of pension and insurance funds need to encourage the matching of assets to liabilities whenever possible.

Finally, if the source of the problem lies in nominal rigidities, whether in accounting practices or 'rule of thumb' investment strategies by institutional investors, regulators and supervisors can highlight their unwonted consequences and potentially act as a catalyst for change.

There has been particular interest since the crisis in the scope for macroprudential policies to head-off financial stability risks. Many countries now have some sort of formal body or committee charged with the task of mitigating financial stability risks (such as the Financial Stability Oversight Council in the US, the European

Systemic Risk Board in the Eurozone, the Financial Policy Committee in the UK, and the Financial Stability Board at the supra-national level). But what are the challenges that need to be faced in deploying such policies? And how much faith should we place in their efficacy?

The first challenge concerns the data. Are there indicators available that can be used reliably to diagnose dangerous financial imbalances at an early stage? After the currency and financial crises in the emerging economies in the 1980s and 1990s, considerable effort was expended in trying to find such a set of indicators, but without much success. The 2007-2008 crisis has prompted a renewed effort to this end. And research such as that by Moritz Schularick and Alan Taylor (2012), together with much work at the Bank for International Settlements, has identified the key role played by excessive credit growth, usually accompanied by asset price booms, in subsequent financial crises and macroeconomic downturns. But the challenge lies in distinguishing between credit growth that is excessive and carries with it risks to future financial stability from credit growth that may be rapid, but is warranted by underlying economic fundamentals.

In one of the more comprehensive recent studies, Giovanni Dell'Ariccia, Deniz Igan, Luc Laeven, and Hui Tong (2012) used data over the past half-century for over 100 countries to examine whether the presence of a credit boom represented a reliable predictor of a future crisis. Using a particular (though intuitively sensible) definition of a credit boom as a period of either rapid growth in the ratio of credit to GDP or an unusual pickup in its rate of growth, they identify no fewer than 175 such episodes. In only one-third of these cases, however, was the credit boom subsequently followed by a financial crisis; what appeared to be a sensible trigger for action actually gave a false positive two-thirds of the time. Of course, further analysis may well generate more reliable diagnostics but this is still very much work in progress. That is in contrast to conventional monetary policymaking, where there is a better understanding – borne of long experience across many countries – of what policy needs to do in order to control inflation.

Second, we are still some way from having a full understanding of the mechanisms that generate a risky 'reach for yield' and thus knowing when such behaviour is unwarranted. Moreover, traditional asset-pricing models provide little guidance as to when such risks are under-priced.[13] Without a convincing theoretical framework, it is difficult to know which macroprudential tools are likely to be most effective. Moreover, market participants will have a financial incentive to look for ways around such interventions, so there will be a tendency for the targeted activities to migrate outside the regulatory perimeter.

Finally, macroprudential tools often involve some form of credit control or credit allocation. Having unelected central bank officials take decisions that clearly impinge on particular parts of the electorate puts the central bank squarely in the political cross hairs. In many countries, elected governments have enacted policies to encourage home ownership through tax breaks, subsidies or the creation of specialised mortgage institutions. If a central bank decides for

---

13 As Larry Summers once noted, financial economics may tell us that the price of a 250 ml bottle of ketchup should be half the price of a 500 ml bottle of ketchup, but it is not very good at telling us what 1 ml of ketchup is worth in the first place.

macroprudential reasons to adopt policies that run counter to those, the central bank's independence risks being called into question, so undermining the credibility and effectiveness of the central bank in its traditional monetary policy role. In turn that may affect a central bank's willingness to deploy such tools.

In summary, macroprudential policies represent a useful addition to central banks' toolkit. But we should be realistic about what they can hope to achieve with them, particularly in a low interest rate environment. We lack good metrics for future risks and have an incomplete understanding of the mechanisms that generate those risks. And the effectiveness of the instruments is still largely unproven. While time and experience may help to fill some of the gaps in our knowledge, for now it is important to avoid a false sense of confidence that macroprudential policies will always be up to the task of preventing financial instability (for more on these and related issues, see Kroszner, 2011, 2012 and 2014).

When financial stability risks cannot be contained by the use of prudential policies, then in principle there may be a case for the focus of monetary policy to shift towards moderating the build-up in financial stability risks, even if it means undershooting the central bank's inflation target for a while, or 'leaning against the wind' (see, for example, Cecchetti et al., 2002; White, 2009). While monetary policy may be a blunt instrument for dealing with financial stability concerns, as Jeremy Stein (2013) notes, by setting the price of leverage it "gets in all cracks".

Of course, it is easy to state this as a principle, but harder to know how to implement it in practice. At what point should central banks start prioritising financial stability concerns ahead of maintaining current demand and stabilising inflation? Running a tighter monetary policy involves incurring certain near-term costs in order to reduce the likelihood or extent of the disruption to activity that may follow future financial instability. A careful cost-benefit analysis is really required so as to assess the net impact on social welfare. One such attempt has recently been provided by Lars Svensson (2014), who finds that in most cases the costs are likely to outweigh the expected benefits: one has to assume either that a tighter monetary policy is very efficacious at discouraging the build-up of risky leverage or that the output losses that arise from financial instability are really very large indeed to make 'leaning against the wind' the right policy.

While there is clearly still much in this area that we do not know, central banks cannot plead ignorance as justification for doing nothing. So when should central banks start at least to contemplate a tighter monetary policy in order to mitigate longer-term financial stability risks? Expansionary monetary policies of both the conventional and unconventional variety can be expected to raise asset prices and boost credit growth; that is part of the transmission mechanism. And asset prices and credit growth are both likely to be unusually low at the depths of a recession, so it clearly would not be right to prevent any rebound whatsoever. But the alarm bells should ring if asset prices rise above a level that would be justifiable in terms of fundamentals if activity, interest rates, and so on, were back to 'normal' levels or debt is so high that a return to normal conditions would force debtholders to de-lever rapidly.

Finally, if financial instability is more likely in a low interest rate world, it puts an even greater premium on ensuring that financial institutions and the financial system are robust. Capital and liquidity regulation, effective resolution regimes and systemic interventions such as ring-fencing all have a role to play. Macroprudential policies should be seen as a complement, not a substitute, for making the financial system more robust (Kroszner and Shiller, 2011; Kroszner, 2012).

The bottom line from all this is that monetary policy is less well suited to the task of keeping aggregate demand in line with potential in an environment where long-term real interest rates hover near zero than was the case during the 1990s when they were around 4%. In the old world, relatively short-lived movements in policy rates were effective at redistributing spending over time and stabilising both activity and inflation. In the new world, prolonged loose policy – even though it may seem warranted by the prevailing natural rate of interest – is more likely to lead financial stability risks to build. It is these risks, rather than the zero lower bound, that may represent the more serious constraint on monetary policy. In essence, the risk-return trade-off for monetary policy looks rather less favourable than it used to. That points to the desirability of other policies – fiscal and structural – shouldering more of the burden.

4.3   Prospects

We now turn to the question posed at the end of Chapter 2: How are risk-free real interest rates likely to evolve in the future? And how might that path be affected by policy choices?

Market participants presently appear to expect very little in the way of a rebound. Figure 4.3 shows ten-year real rates ten years forward for the US and the UK, derived using longer-term TIPS and indexed gilt yields, together with current ten-year spot real rates. For much of the past few years, the real term structure has sloped up. But in recent quarters the forward rates have fallen back noticeably and are only a little higher than the spot rates.

This suggests market participants expect only a very modest rise in real rates from their present historically low levels over at least the next couple of decades. Indeed, it is especially surprising given the lower bound on policy rates, which effectively truncates the lower tail of the distribution of future rates. Given that observed market prices reflect the whole distribution of future rates, it therefore implies that market participants must place relatively little weight on the possibility of higher rates.

Figure 4.3   Spot and forward real yields

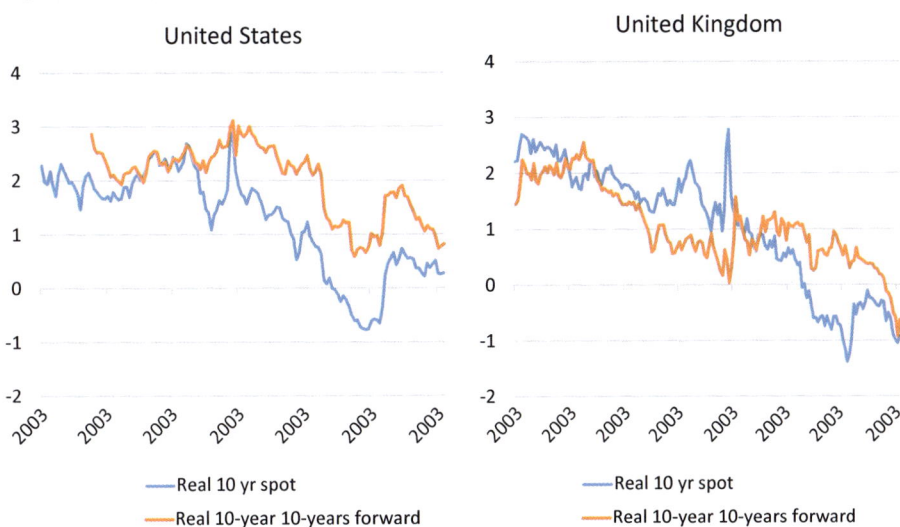

Source: US Federal Reserve Board of Governors and Bank of England.

Were this to be the outcome, it would represent an extraordinary change in the economic environment, implying a natural real interest rate that is zero or below for many years to come. Moreover, as we found in Chapter 1, the only analogous historical period is during the episode of financial repression following World War II, when rates were artificially depressed. While there may some similarities today – in particular, the regulatory pressure on financial institutions to hold a larger share of their assets in a safe and liquid form – it is difficult to believe that we will see the same sort of financial controls that applied then.

Such an outcome would be consistent with the secular stagnation hypothesis. But our analysis of the factors that pressed down on the neutral safe real of rate interest rate in the past also leads us to conclude that there may be rather more of a future rebound than market participants presently appear to expect, although the magnitude and pace at which that will happen remains highly uncertain. As in Chapter 2, we couch our discussion in terms of the main drivers of the supply of savings, the propensity to invest, and the demand and supply of different asset types. We also consider the potential impact that long-term fiscal and structural policies[14] may have on these paths.

---

14 Monetary policy decisions will certainly affect the profile of interest rates in the short run, but should not have a lasting effect on the neutral safe real interest rate in the long run. By the same token, although temporary fiscal policies of stimulus or austerity will certainly affect the current neutral real interest rate, they should not have a durable impact, aside from the effect that the associated change in the path of government debt may have through risk premia. So, for our purposes, it makes more sense to focus attention on the role of long-run fiscal and structural policies.

4.3.1 Shifts in the supply of savings

In Chapter 2, we identified the impact of demographic developments on the supply of savings and the financial integration of China as especially relevant to understanding the downward trend in longer-term real interest rates since the late 1990s.

Beginning with demography, our analysis drew attention to the interaction between saving at different stages of the life-cycle and changes in the size of different age cohorts. On the premise that younger adults spend most of their income and save relatively little, the size of the high-saving middle-aged cohort relative to the size of the dissaving retired is central to the determination of the aggregate propensity to save. And that is consistent with the facts. The period of falling interest rates coincided with a rise in the relative size of the high-saving middle-aged cohort. That has recently peaked, however, as the post-war baby boomers began to pass into retirement and started to run down their accumulated assets. Moreover, the relative size of the middle-aged relative to the retired is set to shrink considerably in the coming decades (see Figure 2.4). Furthermore, both our cross-section analysis (Figure 2.5) and our case study of Japan, where ageing is more advanced (Figure 3.9), supported the thesis that this measure of demographic pressure is related to aggregate savings.

So, other things equal, these demographic shifts point to future upward pressure on the neutral real interest rate from a reduction in the aggregate global propensity to save (in terms of Figure 2.1, the SS curve shifts back). But while the direction of the effect is clear, the timing and magnitude of this shift will depend upon policy choices, as well as economic, social and medical developments.

As already noted in Chapter 2, policies that affect the timing of retirement can have a significant impact on individual household savings behaviour. Increasing the age of eligibility for pension and medical benefits will encourage people to stay in the workforce for longer, reducing the need to save for the future. Also, medical advances allow people to stay healthy and continue working longer. The types of job available may also affect older workers' participation in the labour force, as service-sector jobs tend to require less physical effort than traditional manufacturing jobs. Many older people may also want to stay on in work for the social networking it provides, but working only part-time rather than full-time. Employment legislation that affects the supply of such part-time jobs will therefore matter too. Finally, given the notable contribution of Chinese savings to global savings in recent years, it is worth noting that the development of social insurance there would reduce the incentives for households to self-insure. So even if the basic demographic forces may be relatively impervious to economic policies, the way they are translated into a higher aggregate propensity to save most certainly may be influenced by policy.

Turning to the impact of Chinese financial integration on the world interest rate, this is presumably unlikely to reverse; indeed, it may still have some way to run. It would be a mistake, however, to assume that it will continue to exert downward pressure on global real interest rates. Whether or not that is the case will depend on how the Chinese savings-investment balance evolves, including reserve accumulation by the official sector, as well as whether integration proceeds faster on the savings or investment side of the market. The decline in the Chinese current account surplus already suggests that this factor is likely to be less significant in the future than it has been in the past.

Finally, a brief word on corporate savings is called for. As noted in Chapter 2, even prior to the financial crisis, the net financial asset position of the corporate sector had been rising, both in the US and elsewhere. But that trend accelerated after the 2007-2008 crisis, as businesses reacted to heightened uncertainty and the perception that banks no longer provided a reliable source of finance, by strengthening that financial position further. Some reversal of this recent trend may be expected as the memory of the financial crisis fades, though there seems no particular reason to expect the pre-crisis shift towards higher corporate savings balances to reverse. So this seems likely to provide only modest upward pressure on the natural real interest rate.

To summarise, while some of the factors that contributed to the rise in the supply of savings in the past may persist, the passing through into retirement of the bulge of previously high-saving middle-aged workers in much of the world represents a factor that is likely to reduce significantly the aggregate propensity to save, so exerting upward pressure on the real interest rate. But the precise magnitude and speed at which that takes place is somewhat uncertain, depending in part on policy choices that affect retirement decisions.

4.3.2 Shifts in the propensity to invest

We turn next to factors affecting the propensity to invest. In Chapter 2, we discussed several arguments as to why the propensity to invest might have fallen in recent years, so exerting downward pressure on the natural real interest rate. These included: slower growth in the population of working age; a decline in the rate of innovation; a reduction in the (physical) capital intensity of growth; a fall in the relative price of capital goods; and the after-effects of the financial crisis. We concluded that only the last of these provided a convincing explanation. And it seems plausible that the understandable hesitation on the part of businesses about undertaking new investment following the financial crisis will recede as the recovery proceeds, so adding the upward pressure on the neutral real interest rate coming from the savings side.

But even if investment weakness has not been the main driver of the downward trend in real interest rates since the late 1990s, save perhaps in the period since the financial crisis, it is clear that government policies may nevertheless have a major impact on the propensity to invest going forward. Most significantly, factors such as the rule of law and an ability to enforce contracts are a pre-requisite for companies to be willing to invest. While these may be taken for granted in the advanced economies, they are by no means universal, being weak in some less developed parts of the world. Even if the opportunities for profitable investment are becoming scarcer in the advanced economies, in principle there ought to be plenty of scope for profitable investment in the less developed world, provided those basic factors are present.

Somewhat more mundanely, even in the advanced economies, policy can have an important impact on innovation and businesses' willingness to invest. Low capital taxes increase the return on investment. Governments can fund basic research and use the tax system to encourage private research and development. The design and enforcement of patent law and rules protecting intellectual property is also key. And education and training policies can help to ensure an adequate supply of labour with the skills necessary to exploit new investments is readily available.

Finally, giving businesses a predictable policy environment is important: a constantly changing policy environment makes longer-term planning difficult for businesses and can add significantly to risk premia. Scott Baker, Nicholas Bloom and Steve Davis (2013), for instance, show that measures of policy uncertainty (particularly fiscal and regulatory) have risen since the financial crisis and have discouraged investment. Reducing this uncertainty about policy could also help boost the propensity to invest.

In summary, while we do not find convincing the argument that there has been a long-term decline in new profitable investment opportunities, there are grounds for thinking that heightened uncertainty and the weak recovery after the crisis have discouraged capital formation in recent years. To some extent, the passage of time should cure the problem, but there is also scope for investment- and innovation-friendly policies to hasten a resurgence in the propensity to invest.

4.3.3 Supply of, and demand for, safe versus risky assets

A third set of factors affecting the neutral safe real interest rate concerns the supply of, and demand for, safe[15] versus risky assets. In Chapter 2, we identified several factors that, at different times, have led to an increase in the demand for relatively safe assets. These included, before the crisis, aggressive reserve accumulation by central banks in several emerging economies, especially China. After the crisis, these included: heightened concern on the part of investors about major downside risks; large-scale asset purchases by central banks; and regulatory pressures on financial institutions to hold a larger fraction of their assets in a safe and liquid form.

As far as prospects go, the rate of reserve accumulation by countries such as China has already dropped back; a significant reduction in holdings seems, though, unlikely. Investor concern about extreme downside risks should hopefully fade. The prospect for central bank asset holdings is less clear: the US Federal Reserve and the Bank of England may begin to run down their holdings before too long, but the ECB and the Bank of Japan are still engaged in quantitative easing. Finally, the regulatory pressures on financial institutions to hold more safe assets than before the crisis is sure to be maintained. So there are likely to be somewhat conflicting forces affecting the demand for safe assets.

---

15   Of course, the 2007-2008 crisis and the subsequent Eurozone debt crisis have underscored that what is considered safe constitutes a somewhat movable feast!

As far as the supply of safe assets goes, the financial crisis and subsequent Eurozone debt crisis resulted in certain highly rated structured financial products and peripheral sovereign debt losing their safe status, leading to a marked reduction in the supply of assets that had been perceived to be safe (Table 2.3). That may well have contributed to the rise in risk premia and downward pressure on the safe real rate of interest in the years immediately following the crisis. The opening up of fiscal deficits since the crisis has, however, meant that there has been a sharp increase in issuance of relatively safe sovereign debt. For instance, the gross stock of US government debt outstanding has risen by a quarter since 2008, while it has almost doubled in the UK. Even though central banks have absorbed some of this increase in supply through their quantitative easing programmes, there has nevertheless been an overall increase in the supply of what is presently considered safe sovereign debt. High – though dwindling – levels of issuance will probably be with us for some time, so the supply of safe assets is likely to grow.

Together, the forces on asset demands and supplies perhaps suggest some modest narrowing in risk premia, and thus some correspondingly modest upward pressure on safe rates. But the scale of this effect must be quite uncertain.

4.3.4 Summing up

There are several reasons why it is reasonable to expect the natural real rate of interest to rebound in the future.

- The demographic pressures that have raised the propensity to save since the late 1990s have already begun to move into reverse as the population share of retirees has grown. This looks set to be a strong force depressing aggregate savings propensities over the next few decades.
- The headwinds following the crisis should ease if the recovery strengthens. Firms are likely to become less cautious about investing as uncertainty recedes. And even if the growth in investment opportunities is curtailed in the advanced economies for the reasons cited by the advocates of secular stagnation, there should surely still be plenty of investment opportunities overseas in the emerging and developing world. Balance-sheet repair should also become less pressing for highly indebted households as income growth picks up.
- The portfolio shift towards safe assets could also start to unwind. China is no longer accumulating US Treasuries in the way it did before the crisis. And the preference for safe assets may also begin to lessen as uncertainty recedes and the appetite for risk returns.

But the magnitude and pace of such a reversal in past trends is difficult to predict with any degree of certainty and, moreover, will be influenced by the long-term fiscal and structural policy choices that could either reinforce or offset the forces discussed above.

4.4   Concluding remarks

The present low interest rate environment in the advanced economies is historically most unusual. While the financial crisis has played a part, there also appear to have been more long-standing forces at work, particularly the effect of demographic developments and the integration of China into the global economy. An increase in the demand for safe assets relative to their supply also appears to have played some role.

Were these conditions to persist, they would pose special challenges for individuals and policymakers alike. Central banks would find their ability to vary policy rates would be constrained more often by the lower bound, forcing them to rely instead on less reliable instruments such as quantitative easing. While there are ways to loosen the downside constraint on policy rates, these too have drawbacks. Moreover, an environment of persistently low interest rates is apt to increase the risks to financial stability by encouraging higher leverage and the adoption of excessively risky investment strategies. Prudential policies may be able to mitigate these risks, but we should be wary of expecting too much from relatively untested and potentially controversial policies.

All this makes a return to a world with a higher neutral real interest rate rather desirable. We have argued that this may come about naturally as the demographic forces continue to work through and the after-effects of the financial crisis unwind. But we cannot be certain about either the magnitude or the pace of such a recovery in the neutral real rate. That path is, however, susceptible to the influence of longer-term fiscal and structural policies. Many of those policies – and especially those that raise the prospective return on investment, such as ensuring secure property rights and delivering a stable environment – would be desirable even in the absence of the particular problems associated with persistently low interest rates. But the return from implementing them is all the greater in the present circumstances. And not only would an increased propensity to invest tend to raise the neutral real interest rate, it would also boost growth and thereby ease the burden of debt that still weighs on many households, businesses and governments.

Discussions

Presentation of Chapters 2 and 3

Comments by the discussants

Benoît Coeuré, *European Central Bank*
According to Benoît Coeuré, the report pays justice to the complexity and richness of the different determinants of low interest rates. In particular, the safe assets story is new and important. His discussion focused on three issues. First, there are two possible, contradicting narratives for the low present and future real interest rates and what monetary policy can do about them. The first narrative is related to monetary policy; it is not the main explanation in the report, but it should be part of the discussion. The forward rate is a combination of the expected future rate and the term premium. Monetary policy has contributed to compressing both the expected future rate (through forward guidance) and the term premium (most importantly through QE). The second narrative is a Wicksellian story, implying that the market correctly anticipates that the natural rate will be low for reasons such as low productivity. This is the main theme of the report. From a policy standpoint, these two narratives have different implications. Under the first narrative, monetary policy plays a role in steering real rates into negative territory, which will trigger investment and, in turn, drive real interest rates up. Under the second narrative, the adequate response is structural reforms that increase total factor productivity. Given that the real world is a mixture of both narratives, both accommodative monetary policies that match the decrease of the natural rate *and* structural reforms that push up the real rate are needed.

Second, indeed there are several lessons that Europe can learn from Japan. One is that effective monetary policy requires forward guidance and clear communication on the inflation target. Moreover, the composition of QE matters as much as the quantity. In addition, sequencing of different policies is vital, as QE can only work with a functional bank lending channel and functional banking supervision. Finally, there cannot be a general relaxation of fiscal targets.

The third issue is related to financial stability. Benoît Coeuré was concerned by the conclusion of the report, which might suggest that central banks should give up steering the output gap and inflation and focus on financial stability instead. He disagreed with the recommendation that monetary policy should be geared towards financial stability for two reasons. First, financial stability issues in Europe concern specific sectors and countries, and therefore should be addressed locally. Second, a situation in which monetary policy takes into account financial stability concerns could lead to 'financial dominance'. In conclusion, monetary policy should continue to be geared towards price stability.

Finally, the report should assess the temporary and permanent effects of low interest rates. With respect to the discussion on financial stability, it is important to know at which point low interest rates lead to an irreversible situation in which a flat yield curve pushes part of the financial intermediation into the non-regulated sector and thereby creates financial stability risk.

Lucrezia Reichlin, *London Business School*

Lucrezia Reichlin pointed out that the topic discussed in the report was already important before the Great Recession; it is not related to the crisis, but rather is it linked to long-term trends. The report highlights two potential explanations for the low interest rate environment, namely an increased propensity to save and an increased demand for safe assets. In her discussion, she focused on a third potential explanation – secular stagnation related to a reduction in the propensity to invest – and thereby challenged the main interpretation of the report.

The report stresses that we need to understand the underlying forces driving the natural rate of interest to understand the evolution of the interest rates over the medium term and beyond. Indeed, the natural rate of interest has been declining. We can interpret this as a decline in the world equilibrium interest rate. The authors show that we see a historical decline in nominal yields and that real yields move together across developed markets, implying that we can think of this decline as a single 'world' risk-free rate decline. Post 2008, we have seen a combination of low real rates and low inflation, which is historically unusual. In addition, long-term rates have become less sensitive to changes in policy rates.

The data show that investment-to-GDP ratios in developed markets have been declining. Trends in savings are less clear; saving rates had been fairly stable since the 1980s, declined just prior to the crisis, and have now again stabilised. When quantifying the secular stagnation hypothesis, two issues have to be taken into account. First, the degree of financial integration has changed over time. Second, the intertemporal theory of the current account fails the empirical test if applied to each country separately. To overcome these issues, Reichlin suggested focusing on the G7 economies during the period from 1970 to 2005. China should be excluded from the analysis since it only became financially integrated in the early 2000s, implying that Chinese savings cannot be the driver of the common long-term trend in real rates. Based on this sample, the intertemporal theory of the current account for the joint multi-country behaviour of consumption and the interest rate can be used to determine the equilibrium interest rate in the advanced economies. This multi-country model fits the data well. The estimates since 1970 show both the declining world interest rate and the declining trend in consumption that we observe.

She concluded that the report is too fast to dismiss the secular stagnation hypothesis on the basis of declining investment. A comprehensive empirical analysis should combine the story of declining investment rates with recent developments, such as an increased demand for safe assets and an increased propensity to save in China.

Leslie Teo Eng Sipp, *Government of Singapore Investment Corporation (GIC)*
Leslie Teo Eng Sipp noted that US rates have been at a historic low for many years. Every year both US and global rates have come down, leading to new historic lows. The emphasis of the report on long-term and structural drivers of interest rates is very important. His discussion was centred on five points.

First, a complete understanding of the decline of interest rates and the persistence of low rates would need to blend the supply/demand analysis with cyclical elements. For example, the report should not discount the rise of central bank credibility that came along with the disinflationary regime that began in the 1980s. Moreover, we are living through a period of great deregulation and technological changes. This enables innovation and leads to market globalisation. Also, we have seen the rise of China and other emerging markets, which has affected savings. All of these developments may have worked with the other factors and led to the decline in real interest rates.

Second, we cannot ignore the links between interest rates and financial stability. The credit boom was eventually underpinned by rises in real estate prices in many countries. What may have been a secular decline led to financial and credit excesses, and ultimately resulted in the crisis. This has an effect on where interest rates are today.

Third, rates are low right now, but we should be careful not to extrapolate what markets say about rates. Markets may be under-pricing future developments for two reasons. One is that this has been a prolonged cycle, but otherwise it does not seem to be too different from other financial crises. Another reason is that markets have historically tended to under-price the Fed hike cycle.

Fourth, interest rates are low, but relative pricing of risky assets is not too far from the historical average. Low rates presage low expected returns. The fact that the slope of the capital market line has come down implies lower expected returns. Hence, many investors do not necessarily need to change their asset allocation, as the relative return in terms of asset classes is close to the historic average.

The last point relates to the actions of institutional investors. They have three choices. The first is to stick with existing allocations and to accept lower returns. The second is to move up the risk curve. The third choice is to take on more leverage, for example through strategies like risk parity.

Edwin Truman, *Peterson Institute for International Economics*
Edwin Truman stressed the strengths of this very stimulating report. His remarks were divided into two parts. The first was concerned with the second chapter – the decline of safe real interest rates – while the second part dealt with the third chapter on lessons from Japan's two lost decades.

The challenge in the second chapter is to come up with a consistent story to explain multiple phenomena. Truman was not entirely satisfied with the conclusions of this chapter, for four reasons. First, neither the savings glut hypothesis nor the investment dearth hypothesis explains the stylised facts that investment has fluctuated narrowly and long-term real rates have declined. Second, net private capital flows have been flowing downhill in most regions, except the more advanced emerging markets and the oil-producing countries in the Middle East. However, net official flows dominate the overall results. Excess saving in China is not produced by households, but by the Chinese government as it builds up its reserves. Moreover, it does not seem reasonable that the natural rate of interest in emerging market economies under autarky is lower than in the advanced countries, as suggested in the report. Third, the report exaggerates the role of reserve accumulation by China and other emerging market economies in depressing interest rates on US treasury securities. There is no evidence that China's reserves are primarily invested in US treasuries. Fourth, the analysis on the supply of safe assets that is cited in the report should exclude US mortgage-backed securities and asset-backed securities. Moreover, it is surprising that Japanese and UK sovereign debt is not included in the analysis. Nevertheless, even without the inclusion of these two sovereigns, 'safe assets' rose between 2007 and 2011. In addition, as pointed out by Ben Bernanke, the only true safe assets are claims on central banks. As is well known, the supply of this type of ultimate safe asset is a multiple of what it was in 2007.

In the third chapter on the Japanisation, the authors make a nice distinction between the disinflation period and the deflation period, while emphasising how the former can lead to the latter *inter alia* when downward nominal wage rigidity comes into play. Broad agreement with all six concluding points in the third chapter leaves room for a discussion on emphasis and omissions. First, the experience of Japan shows that a prolonged period of stagnation and low long-term interest rates can occur for reasons that are not captured by the second chapter. Was there a savings and investment story in Japan as well? Second, with respect to monetary policy, it should be stressed that the Bank of Japan did not pursue QE as we now use the term. The focus was on the liability side of the Bank's balance sheet. The expansion was almost exclusively via the purchase of assets very close to maturity rather than focusing on the asset side of the balance sheet and interest rates on longer-term assets. Third, concerning fiscal policy, the report should have put more emphasis on the lack of coordination of monetary and fiscal policy until the advent of Abenomics. Moreover, there was too much emphasis on fiscal retrenchment in the context of continued monetary easing. This resulted in the delay of monetary policy normalisation and consequently little scope to use it during the global crisis. In addition, the report does not clarify whether the build-up of sovereign debt was a risk for Japan and at what point, if at all, the debt-to-GDP ratio became excessive. Fourth, on banking policy, the authors emphasise the importance of the actions and events of 1997-1998 rather than the final cleanup in 2002-2003, which might deserve mention. Likewise, the connection with the Asian financial crisis as indirect and partial global consequences of Japanese policy hesitation, as well as coordinated intervention to support the extremely weak yen, deserves to be brought up. Fifth, turning to the yen's external value, the story during the global crisis and more recently should be more nuanced. It would be useful to look not only at the yen-dollar rate, but also at the yen real effective exchange rate. The latter moved in the same direction, however, only by half as much. The changes in the exchange rate were driven, at least in part, by safe haven attractiveness of the yen.

General discussion

Responding to these comments, **Randall Kroszner** first touched upon the issues that Benoît Coeuré had raised on whether low interest rates are driven by monetary policy or by a Wicksellian view of the natural rate. It is always hard to tell what the natural rate is, yet it is true that resolving this issue is important for policy. In particular, it is necessary to explore whether there are some irreversible aspects of having low interest rates for a prolonged period of time, since we have not experienced such a situation before. As Coeuré mentioned, one possible change is the way in which financial intermediation operates. Indeed, there could be a variety of fundamental changes, such as how financial markets and risk management operate. Concerning macroprudential versus monetary policy, Randall Kroszner argued that it is hard to make a tight distinction. Using macroprudential policy to address particular markets might not be effective. Ultimately, macroprudential policy and monetary policy have to be seen as complements rather than substitutes.

Christian Broda responded to Lucrezia Reichlin that the emphasis on the G7 economies is precisely what the chapter tries to move away from. Certainly, investment rates in the G7 have been falling, but what is particularly important to understand and to incorporate in the analysis is the financial integration between the G7 and the emerging market economies. Given that there are global factors that affect real interest rates in different economies, this is a challenging task. With respect to Edward Truman's comment, he noted that the report highlighted what was happening in 2014, which was a year of fiscal consolidation with little growth. Concerning the debate on fiscal austerity, one should not ignore the experience of Japan from which we learn that it is hard to do fiscal consolidation later on in time.

Takatoshi Ito agreed with Edward Truman that deflation has led to low investment and thus prevented the creation of high quality jobs. With respect to fiscal policy, he argued that Japan must now ensure that the automatic fiscal stabilisers allow for consolidation in good times and for expansionary policies in bad times. Importantly, the budget should balance out over the cycle, which has not been the case so far in Japan.

Part of the subsequent discussion concerned the question of whether low interest rates are driven by monetary policy or whether it is rather a Wicksellian story. **Stefan Gerlach** argued that if the central bank pushes down the actual real interest rate below the Wicksellian real interest rate over a prolonged period of time, the economy should experience tremendous increases in inflation and growth, which does not match recent experience. If, instead, the Wicksellian real interest rate has fallen and the central bank does not react by cutting the policy rate, growth and inflation will slow down, which is what we have seen. Along with formal evidence provided in his own research, Gerlach concluded that the monetary policy hypothesis does not match the empirical regularities, while the Wicksellian story seems to be correct. Following up on this comment, **Luigi Buttiglione** asked whether some asset booms that we have seen during the last two decades, such as the Chinese investment boom, are related to the possibility that interest rates might have been below the Wicksellian rate for some time.

A number of remarks addressed the question of the determinants and evolution of real interest rates. **Richard Baldwin** argued that, in fact, current real rates are not historically low. Rates had been very low in the second half of the 1960s and during substantial parts of the 1970s. Hence, the report should aim at explaining this trend in real rates that starts from the Volcker high rates era and goes on from there.

Jean-Pierre Landau mentioned the numbers that are frequently quoted by Larry Summers on the five-year five-year real expected risk-free interest rate. These numbers suggest that market participants price real returns on treasuries at below 1% and expect this low interest rate environment to continue well into the future. He also wondered about the low sensitivity of investment rates pointed out by Edward Truman. If we believe in the Wicksellian story, what are the factors that inhibit investment and explain the very low interest rates? Similarly, **Luigi Buttiglione** asked whether the report aims to convey the message that interest rates are bottoming out and are expected to go up in the future. **Charles Wyplosz** added that he is troubled that everybody is buying Larry Summers' argument that it all started to decline in the 1990s. The figure by Hamilton et al. (2015) that is presented in the report does not make a very strong case that real interest rates are declining. There might just as well have been a peak in the 1980s, implying that the real interest rate may simply be reverting to the unchanged Wicksellian real interest rate.

Agreeing with Jean-Pierre Landau, **Carlo Monticelli** pointed out that more attention should be devoted to the investment side when thinking about the Wicksellian approach. It is striking that infrastructure investment is extremely low both in advanced and emerging market economies, although liquidity is abundant and interest rates are low. **Anthony Smouha** asked whether the effect of low interest rates on financial intermediation is reversible and where the policy rate should be over the next decade. **Luca Ricci** drew attention to two factors that can impact the evolution of real rates based on a comparison between the pre-crisis period and the post-crisis period. First, depending on how fiscal policy goes forward, there will be upward or downward pressure on interest rates. There are two possible scenarios. One is that there will be a legacy of much higher debt, which should result in higher interest rates when compared to equilibrium. Alternatively, governments will try to build fiscal space, which should lead to downward pressure on interest rates. Second, structural reforms may have an impact on interest rates. The crisis may encourage a lot of structural reforms in Europe, which potentially might lead to a situation in which productivity and investment are higher. **Edmond Alphandery** remarked that the speed at which the savings curve and the investment curve shift right is key to explaining the trend in real interest rates over time. Introducing income into the model could be a way to capture these dynamics. **Claudio Borio** observed that the report puts a lot of emphasis on the cost of deflation. As noted by Raghuram Rajan at a recent conference, current interest rates may be low due to deflation scares. However, work that has been done by the BIS shows that the link between deflation and growth is not that close. **Yi Huang** observed that the Chinese savings rate is mainly driven by corporate savings rather than household savings. The corporate savings rate can be decomposed into the public and the private sector, and it is the latter that determines long-term trends. In China, what matters is financial repression and financial market development. **Tommaso Mancini-Griffoli** noted that income inequality has been commonly mentioned as a driver of a high savings rate and thus of potentially low interest rates. In addition, he argued that there is a disturbing spiral whereby high savings lead to low interest rates, which, in turn, lead to higher precautionary savings. **Gene Frieda** asked the authors about the role that might be given to relative prices in terms of exchange rates as explanatory variables. **Amlan Roy** mentioned the potential role of structural regime shifts and associated asset price instability. He noted that the five-year five-year and the ten-year ten-year forward suggest very different answers.

Several participants commented on the debate concerning safe assets. **Agnès Benassy-Quere** noted that there seems to be an asymmetry between savings and investment in the discussion on safe assets, which neglects the possibility of a shift towards riskier investment. **Gaston Gelos** addressed the view that the demand for a safe assets story is not well supported by credit spreads data when compared to the equity premium. This point is not fully understood yet. There might be institutional reasons behind the shift from equities towards bonds, including riskier bonds. Following up, **Tommaso Mancini-Griffoli** asked to what extend regulation has contributed to the scarcity of safe assets. **Richard Baldwin** suggested looking at the empirical evidence provided by Ricardo Caballero and Emmanuel Farhi (2014). As suggested by Barro (2014), "measuring safe assets in a conceptually meaningful way is a major challenge". The challenge remains, he stated.

With respect to financial integration, **Agnès Benassy-Quere** wondered why the analysis incorporates the notion of a financially integrated savings rate, but not that of a financially integrated investment rate. **Lucrezia Reichlin** replied to Christian Broda concerning the focus on the G7 economies. The narrative in the report is related to the Wicksellian rate, i.e. it is about long-term trends and about the world interest rate. Taking the G7 as an experiment would allow the authors to overcome the issue of financial integration and enable them to explain the downward trend in real rates without bringing the Chinese savings glut into the picture. One can then use the results from such an experiment as a benchmark and incorporate further aspects. **Richard Baldwin** suggested that the authors should include robustness checks on the weights used in the analysis; alternative weights might consider capital controls, domestic credit and liquid assets. **Claudio Borio** noted that it might not be reasonable to refer to capital market integration in a model which is a purely real model without a financial market. **Benoît Coeuré** highlighted the possibility of global disintegration or de-globalisation. In such a situation, trends in either savings or investment in emerging economies may not spill over to advanced economies. Then, developments in emerging markets that point towards an increase in global real rates, such as the turning point in Chinese demography, might not have an impact on real rates in advanced economies. **Luca Ricci** added that it might be the case that a few large economies drive the global interest rate, while emerging markets try to adapt. This heterogeneity could nuance the view on global interest rates.

Jan Marc Berk raised two questions on the chapter on Japan. First, what should policymakers do when both deflation and financial stability risk are prevalent at the same time? Second, he wondered what the lessons from Japan are in the context of a report that is concerned with global developments.

Charles Bean responded to Jean-Pierre Landau's question on the five-year five-year forward interest rates, frequently quoted by Larry Summers. Indeed, the yield curve is incredibly flat. This can be seen by also looking at the ten-year ten-year forward rate, which is virtually the same as the ten-year spot rate. While one might interpret this relationship as an indicator of future interest rate developments, it might also be the case that markets are wrong, as suggested by Leslie Teo Eng Sipp. With respect to Luigi Buttiglione's question, he pointed to several factors that indicate that the Wicksellian rate starts moving back up over time, such as demographic shifts and gradually declining uncertainty. Nonetheless, there is quite some uncertainty concerning the timing of this potential increase in real interest rates. Concerning the discussion on whether monetary policy or the Wicksellian rate have driven the decline in real interest rates, Bean added that it is very difficult to argue that the downward trend is a monetary phenomenon.

Randall Kroszner agreed with the comments made on the low sensitivity of investment to the interest rate. In the aggregate we do not see much responsiveness. This is a fundamental puzzle that requires more attention. With respect to Claudio Borio's remark on deflation, he pointed out that conditionality is an important issue that needs to be explored further. While deflation can be devastating in some cases, it might not be under all circumstances.

Also concerning Claudio Borio's comment, **Christian Broda** noted that allowing for trade linkages implies allowing for capital movements through compensating capital account flows. In that sense, trade might not necessarily be the right measure. On the question of whether low interest rates are a Wicksellian phenomenon, he argued that inflation and growth are a key counterfactual, which, however, is hard to use as we do not know what the counterfactual would have been. He also followed up on Charles Wyplosz's remark. He agreed that there might have been a peak in real interest rates in the 1980s and that the interest rate trend might have started well before. Yet, given insufficiently long series on inflation expectations, it is difficult to evaluate this hypothesis. Highlighting the point made by Gaston Gelos, he noted that indeed there is a very high demand for bonds, which however can be risky or safe.

Takatoshi Ito responded to Jan Marc Berk's comment by noting that lessons from Japan's experience are that if policymakers have to deal with financial stability and deflation at the same time, they should be tough on stress tests, asset quality reviews and recapitalisation and be prepared to inject fiscal money if needed to regain stability. At the same time, monetary policy should be loose to support liquidity and stimulate investment and prevent asset prices from falling too much. With respect to Claudio Borio's remark, he argued that deflation did have adverse effects on investment and consumption in Japan, whereby growth was below potential.

Presentation of Chapters 4 and 5

Comments by the discussants

Claudio Borio, *Bank for International Settlements*
Claudio Borio congratulated the authors for a well-written, clear and comprehensive report. He agreed with many of the policy conclusions that the report reaches, including the following. First, the biggest challenge ahead is how to reconcile monetary and financial stability. Second, the answer to the zero lower bound is not to raise inflation targets, but to prevent financial instability in the first place. Third, monetary policy can contribute to financial booms and busts. Fourth, prudential policy may not be able to deal with financial stability risk on its own, and therefore there is a possible role for monetary policy. Fifth, aggressively repairing banks' balance sheets during a financial bust is critical for the economic recovery and to avoid overburdening monetary policy. Last, monetary policy is less effective in dealing with financial busts and has some undesirable side-effects, not least internationally. Overall, he encouraged the authors to adopt an even more forceful role for monetary policy in preventing financial instability. He made four points.

First, it is not helpful to argue that the natural real interest rate is now lower than it was in the past and that this raises financial stability risks. A lot of credit has to be given to the report for recognising that short-term and long-term rates are set by a combination of central banks' actions and market participants' actions. Unless central banks move the policy rate towards the equilibrium natural rate, the economy experiences a departure from full employment, with inflation going up or coming down. Hence, rising and falling inflation, or even deflation, are key signals that the rate is at the wrong level. However, this is too narrow a notion of an equilibrium rate. If low natural rates generate financial instability, with long-lasting if not permanent effects on output and employment, those rates cannot really be equilibrium rates. This definition reflects the deficiencies in models that do not generate endogenously financial stability. A consequence is that the separation principle, whereby monetary policy should focus only on inflation and output while macroprudential policy deals with financial stability, loses much of its appeal. This is why the separation principle is not particularly helpful when we start from the premise that the task of the central bank is to set the rate at its equilibrium level. The same argument applies to the long-term rate.

Second, it is worth exploring mechanisms through which financial booms and busts have a long-lasting impact on the real economy. Typically, there are two aspects of financial instability. One is a pure financial aspect; the other is the real aspect. The key is how the two interact. However, we tend to treat the two separately. In addition, we pay a lot of attention to the financial aspects and too little attention to the real aspects that are associated with financial booms and busts. Some work done at the BIS has shown that financial booms tend to undermine productivity growth. A considerable part of this takes place through the shift of factors of production to lower productivity sectors. In addition, the larger the misallocations during the financial boom, the bigger the cumulative fall in productivity after a financial crisis strikes. It calls for revisiting the notion that for any policy-relevant horizon, money is neutral. Moreover, it is worth broadening the mechanisms behind hystereses to include those that take place through the misallocation of resources. The role of misallocations highlights the limitations of expansionary monetary policy during financial busts. The bottom line is that not all output gaps are born equal and are amenable to the same kind of remedies.

Third, there is a risk of a possible unsustainable path of monetary policy, i.e. a complementary explanation for the decline in real rates. There are two interpretations of the long-term decline in interest rates. These are not mutually exclusive, but rather complementary. One is that the policy interest rate follows where the natural rate is going. The other one is that asymmetric monetary policy responses over successive financial and business cycles have failed to lean against unsustainable financial booms and busts, which cause long-term damage to the real economy. Consequently, policy responds very aggressively and persistently. Over time, this response imparts a downward bias to interest rates and an upward bias to debt levels. At some point it becomes harder to raise rates without causing damage, because debt levels are too high and because the system becomes accustomed to these very low rates. Hence, to some extent, low rates become self-validating. Too low rates in the past are a reason why we see such low rates today.

Finally, monetary policy frameworks need greater tolerance for deviations of inflation from target. Strong and valid objections to a more forceful use of monetary policy in preventing financial booms and busts must be carefully assessed. One objection is that it is difficult to identify financial imbalances. Yet, a whole set of macroprudential policies are based on that premise. Another objection is that monetary policy has limited impact on financial risk taking. As the report suggests, that is not quite right. In fact, monetary policy operates through many channels that are the same as those of macroprudential policies when it comes to restraining financial booms. The biggest issue is how to reconcile a more forceful use of monetary policy with current mandates. This requires greater tolerance for deviation from inflation targets.

Fritz Zurbruegg, *Swiss National Bank*
Fritz Zurbruegg emphasised that the report brings together a lot of things that we have been reading over the last couple of years and that it highlights nicely some of the main challenges monetary policymakers are facing. His comments focused on the short-term monetary policy instruments that have been used in Switzerland.

Zurbruegg first pointed out the need to emphasise the real aspects. If we assume that the Wicksellian rate is linked to the growth potential of the economy, it would make sense to further discuss the option of boosting growth potential with structural reforms, given the importance for the real interest rate.

Next, he looked at the zero lower bound and unconventional monetary policy instruments. A small number of central banks have now gone further and are questioning whether the zero lower bound is binding. The Swiss National Bank started by decreasing rates to -25 basis points in December 2014. Following the lifting of the exchange rate floor, it further decreased the rate to -75 basis points, thus pushing the limit of negative deposit rates. This move was extremely important to at least partially compensate for the tightening bias from the appreciation of the Swiss franc.

The report mentions that while this is desirable from a monetary policy perspective, there are some issues concerning financial stability and cash substitution. At -75 basis points, the rate is slightly beyond the report's figure for the tipping point for cash substitution of -50 basis points, which is also suggested by the Swiss National Bank's own work. However, this tipping point is not clearly defined; markets and businesses are very innovative, which implies that any *ex ante* rate that defines the tipping point is not set in stone. As flagged by the report, an important aspect to keep in mind is that people become extremely innovative in compressing their non-negligible cost of holding cash. Another aspect is related to the duration of negative interest rates. As there is an initial fixed cost of moving large amounts of cash, the average cost is lower the longer those costs can be amortised. Hence, the longer the expected duration of negative rates, the higher the probability of cash substitution.

The issue of financial stability is very clearly highlighted in the report. One important question is what happens to real estate price developments and mortgage loan growth if rates are pushed even further below zero. Interestingly, since the introduction of negative rates in Switzerland, mortgage rates and the rates for some firm loans have been increasing instead of decreasing. This is related to hedging costs and the fact that most Swiss banks are not willing to pass on negative rates to retail deposits. In addition, banks are under pressure to maintain profit margins in the face of low interest rates. Banks can either raise the lending volume or increase maturity transformation. Both of these options lead to higher risk taking and more financial stability risk.

Finally, going from zero rates to negative rates has caused political pressure in a non-linear way. Issues that are unrelated to monetary policy have suddenly been linked to the Swiss National Banks' policy. For example, pension funds have had structural issues for a long time. These have become even more relevant with the introduction of negative rates and therefore resulted in significant pressure to adjust monetary policy, at least in Switzerland. Moreover, negative rates have sparked a public debate about the cost of potentially negative savings deposit rates. This has become a political issue, putting a lot of pressure on the Swiss National Bank. The irrational component that comes into play when going from zero to negative rates cannot be underestimated.

Kiyohiko Nishimura, *Tokyo University*

Kiyohiko Nishimura noted that the report provides a good summary of the issued involved with low interest rates. He broadly agrees with the authors' conclusions. One point to add is that monetary policy is not simply an economic decision but also a political one. For Japan, for instance, international pressure concerning the exchange rate made it impossible to engage in aggressive QE.

His discussion aimed at providing a different perspective on the issue of low interest rates. Lowering policy rates has become ineffective at boosting growth, even if rates hit zero or are in negative territory. This is the consequence of the composite effect of three simultaneous global 'seismic' shifts. First is the persistent fallout from the so-called great property bubbles/busts and financial crisis. The collapse of a property bubble has long-lasting effects; it hampers financial intermediation and results in weak demand, which becomes less responsive to traditional monetary policy. Thus, it is of utmost importance to avoid property bubbles, as has also been stressed by the authors in the report.

The second shift is the employment-unfriendly impact of ubiquitous information and communication technology. Information and communication technology has substantially reduced the number of medium-skilled jobs in developed countries. This reduces labour income growth, which is one traditional mechanism of monetary policy transmission. It also reduces labour market flexibility and efficiency. This issue will soon become global, since information and communication technology is increasingly easy to access.

Third, many economies have experienced a shift from a demographic bonus to a demographic onus. A demographic bonus often causes excessive optimism. If this excessive optimism is combined with financial innovation and easy credit, a credit cycle of boom and bust will result. A shift from demographic bonus to onus often coincides with the turning point from excessive optimism to excessive pessimism. People's expectations become a very important determinant of demand. This concerns asset prices and growth and goes well beyond inflation expectations.

Right now, we are in the stage of rebuilding from the systemic damages of the past property bubbles and are still in the transition phase concerning both demographic developments and information and communication technology. Therefore, we face heightened uncertainty and we have to think about the difference between growing out of the crisis and bubbling out of the crisis. We also have to be aware of the side-effects of QE, which reduces the price discovery capacity of the market, something that is crucial when there is substantial uncertainty. The central bank has a vital role as an information provider. It has the responsibility of drawing attention to the importance of fundamentals and of understanding risks even when some policy prescriptions are not purely central bank related. Central bank policies should be examined from this perspective, whereby the central bank is a credible provider of information in the framework of financial stability, as is emphasised in the report.

Thomas Huertas, *Ernst & Young*

Commenting on regulatory aspects, Thomas Huertas asked whether fixing finance will fix the transmission mechanism. As is well known, policy is only one part of the picture. Without a sound transmission mechanism, policy will be ineffective. In the Great Moderation we all assumed that – at least for macroeconomic policy – the transmission mechanism was stable. We got stable growth and low inflation, and monetary policy advocates modestly laid claim to the success of the Great Moderation. In the crisis, the transmission mechanism proved unstable. There are various theories as to why this is the case, including inherent risk taking on the part of banks, sudden changes in support by the US government, and the previous departure from the Taylor rule by the Fed in the years leading up to the crisis. In response to the crisis, there was massive monetary and fiscal stimulus. Rates changed by four and a half percentage points in the UK and two percentage points in the US, and much of the change occurred in the immediate aftermath of the crisis. The financial sector has been under reform ever since. This has implications for the transmission mechanism.

There is a massive regulatory programme under way to make the system robust and fix finance. The programme entails making banks safer through capital and liquidity requirements. Moreover, it makes derivatives clearing mandatory, assures that central counterparty clearing houses are robust, controls shadow banking, strengthens insurance regulation, and enforces review of asset management. In addition, an overlay of macroprudential supervision is imposed as a backstop to microprudential regulation. The reform programme has certainly strengthened the banking system and the overall financial system. Nonetheless, some issues remain and many of these policy tools are as yet untested. For example, banking is linked very concretely to the asset prices of houses and the question of loan-to-value ratios. This is a sensitive issue and it is not yet clear whether it is going to be directly or indirectly regulated. Thomas Huertas focused on two issues that have broad implications.

First, the transmission mechanism has traditionally been associated with banks. The tendency of the reform and of market developments, however, has been to reduce the role of banks in the financial system. In terms of macroeconomic and financial stability policy, one needs to analyse the question of whether banks are still big enough to serve as a transmission mechanism. If not, what is the alternative? The logical alternative is capital markets, but some elements of banking and capital markets regulation may undermine their ability to fulfil that transmission role.

Second, market liquidity is declining in the sense that the ability to buy and sell bonds in large amounts without influencing the price is diminishing. In part this is due to capital demands on the inventory. While one could dismiss this as industry pleading, it is an issue that merits investigation.

We need a transmission mechanism. It is not clear what is it going to look like and where it is going to come from. However, if we aim at having financial stability, we need a stable transmission mechanism.

General discussion

Christian Broda acknowledged the lack of symmetric monetary policy response highlighted by Claudio Borio. He also agreed that there are international monetary policy spillovers from the larger to the smaller economies, such as Switzerland. However, he questioned whether this report is the right framework to address this issue.

In response to Claudio Borio, **Takatoshi Ito** noted that productivity growth in Japan was respectable compared to the US and that consumption and investment decisions were based on deflationary expectations. Hence, he concluded, Japan could have done better by preventing deflation to set in. He agreed that smaller economies, such as Japan and Switzerland, suffered from spillovers due to safe haven effects when other advanced economies' central banks engaged in QE. Monetary policy in Japan became too tight at the time.

Responding to Thomas Huertas, who mentioned that the Financial Policy Committee at the Bank of England was reluctant to ask for directive power over loan-to-value ratios, **Charles Bean** indicated that the Committee has just made such a request. It did not do so earlier because it was not clear whether there would be sufficient public support. Concerning Claudio Borio's remarks, he agreed that financial stability concerns may warrant deviations from the inflation target. The real question, however, is not so much the mandate but whether there would be public support for running a period of relatively tight policy when unemployment is going up on the grounds that it is necessary to head off financial stability risks. Regardless of whether it concerns macroprudential instruments or monetary policy, it is important to build a constituency for financial stability in the same way as central banks have built a constituency for price stability.

Alexander Swoboda wondered whether the report's general conclusions depend on the situation in each country at any point in time. In the same vein, **Ludovít Ódor** wondered about the Eurozone, where there is not much fiscal space and structural policies are politically problematic. Does this mean that we should expect a sort of 'Japanisation' in Europe? Similarly, **Carlo Monticelli** asked for more discussion of fiscal policy: what should governments do to make the most of this period of low interest rates, and what does it imply for the composition of public spending?

Concerning fiscal policy, **Tommaso Mancini-Griffoli** suggested a cost-benefit analysis of using monetary policy to reduce financial stability risk. He mentioned the idea of applying the separation principle – monetary policy focuses on price stability, macroprudential policy is in charge of financial stability – unless asset prices and credit reach a certain threshold. The problem with this idea, however, is that once the threshold is reached, it might be too late for monetary policy to react. **Hans Genberg** followed up by drawing attention to a new IMF database on the use of macroprudential policies in over 100 countries for the period from 2000 to 2013, which shows a number of patterns. First, there is an increasing use of macroprudential tools in all regions of the world. Second, and more importantly, there are multiple instruments now in place in many countries. The overall effect of this proliferation of instruments may be quite difficult to assess. Third, the introduction of macroprudential instruments seems to be permanent;

once they are introduced, they do not seem to be phased out. While this may just be a feature of the particular period (2000-2013), it could also be an indication that these policies are part of increasing regulation and, ultimately, financial repression.

Peter Praet was struck by the fact that the term premium is negative, implying that the short-term real rate is higher than it would be in the absence of this term premium. He also invited the authors to further examine why long-term investment is so weak in view of extremely low rates. On this issue, **Mathias Hoffmann** observed that only big private borrowers and public borrowers can access credit at low rates, leaving a large part of the private sector, such as small and medium-sized enterprises, unable to borrow at all or facing infinite borrowing rates. Do lower rates lead to distorted signals? It might well be that, in an environment of low rates, banks have no incentive to clean up their balance sheets, which is required for them to lend to smaller, bank-dependent firms again. **Anne Le Lorier** mentioned that there are many angles on low interest rates. One that is particularly important for the Eurozone at this juncture is the impact on debt sustainability. It is important to make a link between low rates and debt sustainability at a time when rebuilding a fiscal buffer is a priority. She also wondered about a possible impact of prudential regulation on productivity and growth. This led her to conclude that it is important to look at the alignment of incentives in the financial sector with the needs of the real economy. On her first observation, **Charles Wyplosz** opined that it might be wrong to call for fiscal stabilisation in the wake of financial stability, and even more detrimental to refrain from raising rates because of debt sustainability constraints.

Amlan Roy argued that it is not the short rate that mattes, but the yield curve. The long end of the yield curve is controlled by insurance companies, pension funds and re-insurance companies. **Laura Kodres** suggested three aspects that might be worthwhile exploring closely. First, on the savings rate, the report could explore who is saving and why. Are savings driven by households, governments or corporates? Do these actors save for intertemporal consumption smoothing or for precautionary reasons? It might be the case that the two motives are no longer clearly separable: as they face high uncertainty, young people are inclined to save and not to borrow. She also noted that corporate bond issuance is at a record high and yet there is hardly any corporate investment. Most of the bond issuance goes into mergers and acquisitions. An essential question is why corporates do not invest more and whether this is related to uncertainty. She also revisited the monetary transmission mechanism – banks are stepping away, whereas non-banks are stepping in. In part, this is due to regulations on banks that inhibit maturity and credit transformation. Should we really be thinking of monetary policy as going only through banks? This matters for financial stability. On the same point, **Anthony Smouha** added that in the UK there is a lot of criticism that banks are not lending because they are raising their capital ratios.

More generally, **Ivan Adamovich** commented on the political economy implications of negative interest rates. It is easy for central banks to lower interest rates while still in positive territory. It becomes more complicated when reaching negative territory, as the public and politicians might not support that decision.

This leads to the question of central bank independence. **Jean-Pierre Landau** observed that some people made the case that the rates projected by the market are wrong, implying that rates might go up earlier than indicated by markets. In view of Kiyohiko Nishimura's argument that technological changes lead to uncertainty in the labour market, he wondered whether reduced worker power could prolong the low interest rate period. On the issue of search for yield, *Tommaso Mancini-Griffoli* noted that we used to think of this phenomenon as something that affected mainly pension funds. As mentioned by Fritz Zurbruegg, however, bank profits might turn negative when interest rates hit zero and thus there might be an incentive for banks to reach for yield as well. **Luca Ricci** asked how feasible it is to keep interest rates in negative territory for some time and whether they could be pushed further down, for example as far as -2%. He linked the discussion on global interest rates to the debate on macroprudential policies versus monetary policy. The link, he argued, could either lead us to conclude that there are limits on how freely exchange rates can float (the dilemma versus trilemma situation described by Hélène Rey), or instead that monetary policy independence can only be established through a flexible exchange rate regime (as argued by Maurice Obstfeld).

Closing the conference, the authors replied to the last round of remarks. In response to Alexander Swoboda, **Charles Bean** reiterated his view that the risk-return trade-off for monetary policy is less attractive in this environment of very low interest rates. A corollary is that it is worth trying macroprudential policies while other policymakers need to simultaneously think about other options, such as structural and fiscal policies. Concerning Jean-Pierre Landau's remark on the power of labour, he answered that the evolution of workers' power might depend on where one is on the skills distribution. Highly skilled workers have found their market power increasing whereas medium-skilled and low-skilled workers have been losing market power due to technological changes. This might indeed have implications for aggregate savings rates through changes in the distribution of income. He agreed with Ivan Adamovich that the political economy of central banks is going to become more difficult. The policy territory that has been entered when engaging in QE inevitably exposes central banks to more political pressures. Pre-crisis, central banks just focused on inflation targeting and there was public acceptance of the distributional consequences that went along with temporary variations in interest rates. This is not the case when interest rates are perceived as deviating from normal levels for a long time. Similarly, macroprudential policies, often under the roof of the central bank, are inevitably very political. Why are companies not investing? There are two alternative answers to this question. One possibility could be that uncertainty is still high. The alternative view is related to the secular stagnation hypothesis, which would imply that investment could remain permanently depressed.

In response to Jean-Pierre Landau's remark, **Takatoshi Ito** argued that not only technology but also cheaper labour in emerging economies is replacing low-skilled jobs in advanced economies. This is a structural problem that cannot be addressed by monetary policy. With respect to the question on demography, he explained that in a closed-economy Solow growth model, a decline in labour would entail a decline in capital and investment through a drop in the real interest rate. In an open economy, there are other, profound implications on interest rates and investment that need to be fleshed out. Concerning the comment on the political economy aspect of monetary policy raised by Ivan Adamovich, he mentioned that this is precisely why an inflation-targeting framework is valuable. Being explicit about the medium-run target is important both for the anchoring of inflation expectations and for political cover. On the question from Luca Ricci on whether there is a limit to how negative interest rates can go, he expressed the view that there is a lower bound, but precisely where it is does not matter. If rates were below the lower bound, some fundamental changes would probably occur. Concerning the remarks on debt sustainability and fiscal policy, he added that low interest rates might lead to moral hazard for governments. It should be clear, however, that rates are kept low to revive the economy and achieve the inflation target, and that this should not be exploited by governments to postpone tax increases or expand debt.

Christian Broda noted that term premia is a way to decompose short-term and long-term rates, but the fact that many countries have negative term premia goes directly against our intuition. In response to Mathias Hoffmann, he argued that part of the reason why there has been no recovery in lending comes from the tension between deleveraging and re-leveraging. The current low interest rate environment gives banks the incentive to re-lever, but the system has not been cleaned up yet. This also relates to the point on fiscal policy raised by Carlo Monticelli, where we also see some tension. We need to act countercyclically, which involves having primary surpluses prior to a crisis. Hence, the debate should not only focus on fiscal austerity today but also on the next cycle. Finally, with respect to banking performance, he added that periods of deleveraging require subsidies through very low interest rates. The issue here is that QE has changed the relationship between banks and net interest margin securities. One option is to recapitalise banks through a steeper yield curve. However, attacking the long end of the curve and bringing down term premia prevents this from happening. This observation also relates to the discussion on why QE might have been less powerful than expected.

References

Armenter, R. (2012), "The Rise of Corporate Savings", *Philadelphia Business Review*, Third Quarter.

Baker, S., N. Bloom and S. Davis (2013), "Measuring Economic Policy Uncertainty," Chicago Booth Working Paper No. 13-02, University of Chicago Booth School of Business.

Barro, R. (2006), "Rare disasters and asset markets in the Twentieth Century", *Quarterly Journal of Economics* 121(3), pp. 823-866.

_____ (2009), "Rare disasters, asset prices, and welfare costs", *American Economic Review* 99(1), pp. 243–264.

Bank of England (2013), Letter to Andrew Tyrie, Chairman of Treasury Committee, 16 May (available at http://www.parliament.uk/documents/commons-committees/treasury/130516-C.pdf).

Bank for International Settlements (BIS) (2015), *Annual Report*, Basel, Switzerland, June.

Bernanke, B.S. (2005), "The global saving glut and the U.S. current account deficit", Sandridge Lecture, Virginia Association of Economists, 14 April.

_____ (2015), "WSJ Editorial Page Watch: The Slow-Growth Fed?", Brookings, 30 April (http://www.brookings.edu/blogs/ben-bernanke/posts/2015/04/30-wsj-editorial-slow-growth-fed).

Blanchard, O., G. Dell'Ariccia and P. Mauro (2010), "Rethinking macroeconomic policy", *Journal of Money, Credit and Banking* 42(s1), pp. 199–215.

Broadbent, B. (2014), "Monetary policy, asset prices and distribution", Speech to the Society of Business Economists, 23 October.

Broda, C. and D. Weinstein (2005), "Happy News from the Dismal Science: Reassessing Japanese Fiscal Policy and Sustainability," in T. Ito and D. Weinstein (eds), *Solutions to Japan's Problems*, Cambridge, MA: MIT Press.

Brynjolfsson, E. and A. McAfee (2011), *Race Against the Machine: How the Digital Revolution is Accelerating Innovation, Driving Productivity, and Irreversibly Transforming Employment and the Economy*, Digital Frontier Press.

Buiter, W. (2009), "Negative nominal interest rates: Three ways to overcome the zero lower bound", NBER Working Paper No. 15118, Cambridge, MA.

Buttiglione, L., P. Lane, L. Reichlin and V. Reinhart (2014), *Deleveraging, What Deleveraging?*, Geneva Reports on the World Economy 16, Geneva: ICMB and London: CEPR.

Caballero, R. and E. Farhi (2014), "On the role of safe asset shortages in secular stagnation", in C. Teulings and R. Baldwin (eds), *Secular Stagnation: Facts, Causes and Cures*, A VoxEU eBook, London: CEPR Press.

Cecchetti, S., H. Genberg and S. Wadhwani (2002), "Asset Prices in a Flexible Inflation Targeting Framework", in W. Hunter, G. Kaufman and M.

Pomerleano (eds), *Asset Price Bubbles: The Implications for Monetary, Regulatory and International Policies*, Cambridge, MA: MIT Press.

Cowen, T. (2011), *The Great Stagnation: How America Ate All The Low-Hanging Fruit of Modern History, Got Sick, and Will (Eventually) Feel Better*, New York: Dutton Press.

Cowen, T. and R.S. Kroszner (1994), *Explorations in the New Monetary Economics*, New York: Blackwell Publishers.

Dell'Ariccia, G., D. Igan, L. Laeven and H. Tong, with B. Bakker and J. Vandenbussche (2012), "Policies for Macrofinancial Stability: How to Deal with Credit Booms," IMF Staff Discussion Note, Washington, DC, 7 June.

Eggertsson, G.B. and M. Woodford (2003), "The zero bound on interest rates and optimal monetary policy", *Brookings Papers on Economic Activity* 1, pp.139–211.

Eichengreen, B. (2014), "Losing interest", *Project Syndicate*, 11 April.

Eisler, R. (1932), *Stable Money, The Remedy for the Economic World Crisis: A Programme of Financial Reconstruction for the International Conference 1933*, London: The Search Pub Co.

Gagnon, J., M. Raskin, J. Remache and B. Sack (2010), "Large-Scale Asset Purchases by the Federal Reserve: Did They Work?", Federal Reserve Bank of New York Staff Report No. 441.

Gerlach, S. and L. Moretti (2014), "Monetary policy and TIPS yields before the Crisis", *The B.E. Journal of Macroeconomics* 14(1), pp. 689-701.

Gesell, S. (1916), *Die Natürliche Wirtschaftsordnung*, Rudolf Zitzmann Verlag, available in English as *The Natural Economic Order*, London: Peter Owen Ltd (1958).

Goldfajn, I. and R. Valdes (1999), "The Aftermath of Appreciations", Quarterly *Journal of Economics* 114(1), pp. 229-262.

Gordon, R.J. (2012), "Is U.S. economic growth over? Faltering innovation confronts the six headwinds", NBER Working Paper No. 18315, Cambridge, MA.

_____ (2014), "The demise of U.S. economic growth: Restatement, rebuttal and reflections", NBER Working Paper No. 19895, Cambridge, MA.

Greenspan, A. (2005), "Testimony of Chairman Alan Greenspan", Committee on Banking, Housing and Urban Affairs, U.S. Senate.

Hamilton, J., E. Harris, J. Hatzius and K. West (2015), "The Equilibrium Real Funds Rate: Past, Present and Future", mimeo.

Hansen, A. (1939), "Economic progress and declining population growth", *American Economic Review* 29(1), pp. 1-15.

Hoshi, T. and T. Ito (2013), "Is the Sky the Limit? Can Japanese Government Bonds Continue to Defy Gravity?", *Asian Economic Policy Review* 8, pp. 218-247.

_____ (2014), "Defying Gravity: can Japanese sovereign debt continue to increase without a crisis?", *Economic Policy* 77, pp. 5-44.

IMF (2015), *Global Financial Stability Report*, Washington, DC, April.

Jorgenson, D., M. Ho and J. Samuels (2014), "What will revive U.S. economic growth? Lessons from a prototype industry-level production account for the United States", working paper, Harvard University, February.

Joyce, M., A. Lasaosa, I. Stevens and M. Tong (2011), "The financial market impact of quantitative easing", *International Journal of Central Banking* 7(3), pp. 113–161.

Justiniano, A. and G.E. Primiceri (2010), "Measuring the Equilibrium Real Interest Rate", *Economic Perspectives* 34(1), pp. 14–27, Federal Reserve Bank of Chicago.

Karabarbounis, L. and B. Neiman (2012), "Declining Labor Shares and the Global Rise of Corporate Savings", Booth School of Business Working Paper, University of Chicago, October.

King, M. and D. Low (2014), "Measuring the 'world' real interest rate", NBER Working Paper No. 19887, Cambridge, MA.

Krishnamurthy, A. and A. Vissing-Jorgensen (2011), "The Effects of Quantitative Easing on Interest Rates: Channels and Implications for Policy", *Brooking Papers on Economic Activity* 43(2), pp. 215-287.

_____ (2013), "The Ins and Outs of Large-Scale Asset Purchases", in *Global Dimensions of Unconventional Monetary Policy*, Federal Reserve Bank of Kansas City.

Kroszner, R.S. (2011), "Challenges for Macro-Prudential Supervision", in S. Claessens, D. Evanoff, G. Kaufman and L. Kodres (eds), *Macroprudential Regulatory Policies: The New Road to Financial Stabilty?*, Hackensack, NJ: World Scientific Publishers, pp. 379-86.

_____ (2012), "Stability, Growth, and Regulatory Reform", in *Financial Stability Review: Public Debt, Monetary Policy, and Financial Stability*, Paris: Banque de France, pp. 87-93.

_____ (2014), "Fire Extinguishers and Smoke Detectors: Macroprudential Policy and Financial Resiliency", *Banking Perspectives* 2(4), pp. 16-20.

Kroszner, R.S. and R. Shiller (2011), *Reforming U.S. Financial Markets: Before and Beyond Dodd-Frank*, Cambridge, MA: MIT Press.

Lo, S. and K. Rogoff (2015), "Secular stagnation, debt overhang and other rationales for sluggish growth, six years on", BIS Working Paper No. 482, Basel.

Mian, A. and A. Sufi (2014), *House of Debt: How They (and You) Caused the Great Recession, and How We Can Prevent It from Happening Again*, Chicago, IL: University of Chicago Press.

Miles, D. (2014), "The transition to a new normal for monetary policy", Speech given at the Mile End Group, Queen Mary College, London, 27 February.

Moessner, R., D.-J. Janssen and J. de Haan (2015), "Communication about future policy rates in theory and practice: A survey", DNB Working Paper No. 475, Amsterdam.

Mokyr, J. (2013), "Is technological progress a thing of the past?", VoxEU.org, 8 September.

OECD (2011), "Pensionable Age and Life Expectancy, 1950-2050", in *Pensions at a Glance 2011: Retirement Income Systems in OECD and G20 Countries*, Paris: OECD Publishing.

Reifschneider, D. and J. Williams (2000), "Three lessons for monetary policy in a low inflation era", *Journal of Money, Credit and Banking* 32(4), pp. 936-966.

Reinhart, C. and K. Rogoff (2009), "The Aftermath of Financial Crises", *American Economic Review* 99(2), pp. 466-472.

_____ (2010), "Growth in a time of debt", *American Economic Review* 100(2), pp. 573–578.

Reinhart, C. and B. Sbrancia (2015), "The Liquidation of Government Debt", IMF Working Paper 15/7, Washington, DC.

Rudebusch, G. (2009), "The Fed's monetary policy response to the current crisis", Federal Reserve Bank of San Francisco Economic Letter No. 2009-17.

Schularick, M. and A.M. Taylor (2012), "Credit booms gone bust: Monetary policy, leverage cycles, and financial crises, 1870-2008", *American Economic Review* 102(2), pp. 1029-61.

Solt, F. (2014), "The Standardized World Income Inequality Database", Working Paper, SWIID Version 5.0, October.

Stein, J. (2013), "Overheating in credit markets: Origins, measurement, and policy responses", Speech at the "Restoring Household Financial Stability after the Great Recession: Why Household Balance Sheets Matter" research symposium sponsored by the Federal Reserve Bank of St. Louis, 7 February.

Summers, L. (2013), Remarks at the IMF Fourteenth Annual Research Conference, 8 November.

_____ (2014), "U.S. economic prospects: Secular stagnation, hysteresis, and the zero lower bound", *Business Economics* 49(2).

Svensson, L.E.O. (2015), "Inflation targeting and leaning against the wind", forthcoming in *Fourteen Years of Inflation Targeting in South Africa and the Challenge of a Changing Mandate*, Pretoria: South African Reserve Bank.

Teulings, C. and R. Baldwin (2014), *Secular Stagnation: Facts, Causes and Cures*, A VoxEU eBook, London: CEPR Press (available at http://www.voxeu.org/content/secular-stagnation-facts-causes-and-cures).

Thwaites, G. (2014), "Why are real interest rates so low? Secular stagnation and the relative price of investment goods", mimeo.

White, W. (2009), "Should Monetary Policy 'Lean or Clean'?", Federal Reserve Bank of Dallas Globalisation and Monetary Policy Institute Working Paper No. 34.

Williams, J. (2014), "Monetary policy at the zero lower bound: Putting theory into practice", Hutchins Center on Fiscal and Monetary Policy, Brookings Institution, Washington DC.

Woodford, M. (2012), "Methods of policy accommodation at the interest-rate lower bound", in *The Changing Policy Landscape*, Federal Reserve Bank of Kansas City.